*SCENES FROM THE PAST: 29 (PART F*

# STEAM OVER WOODH

## ---- PART ONE ----

# MANCHESTER LONDON ROAD via GORTON & GUIDE BRIDGE to HADFIELD and including the FALLOWFIELD LINE

**Godley Junction, c.1936:** Godley Junction was one of the important focal points on the Woodhead line. Here traffic over the CLC from industrial Merseyside was received, dispatched and interchanged. In a splendid vintage scene B7 No.5034 pulls away from the CLC platforms and joins the GC main line with an Up excursion working numbered 348. A 12-coach train, the stock includes some GWR vehicles and is, possibly, an excursion from the Liverpool area to one of the East Coast seaside resorts. In the sidings behind the signalbox another B7 - in the number series 31-35 awaits further duties. Worthy of mention is the splendid assortment of signals with both lattice and solid posts. *William Lees*

***E.M.JOHNSON***

# STEAM OVER WOODHEAD
## - PART ONE -
## MANCHESTER LONDON ROAD VIA GORTON & GUIDE BRIDGE TO HADFIELD AND INCLUDING THE FALLOWFIELD LINE

ISBN 978-1-909625-12-9

FIRST PUBLISHED 2013

PRINTED BY THE AMADEUS PRESS
CLECKHEATON BD19 4TQ
PUBLISHED BY BOOK LAW PUBLICATIONS
382 CARLTON HILL NOTTINGHAM NG4 1JA

**DEDICATION:** It gives me great pleasure to dedicate this book to the next generation of the Johnson family, my dear and lovely grandchildren: Cian Michael, Sophie May, Shea Daniel, Erin Rose and Orla Lou.

# Foreword

The last volume in my Woodhead trilogy was entitled "Woodhead, the Electric Railway." Good fortune, via Andrew Claxton's generosity in allowing me access to his father's papers, notes and photographs, brought to publication hitherto unknown facts regarding the development of electric loco No.6000, latterly known as *Tommy.*

And though the Woodhead line, to the modern generation at least, is known and fondly remembered as a more or less purely electric railway, it is pertinent to remember that this iconic route was steam-powered for well over a century, much more than a lifetime. With this in mind I can promise the reader a generous helping of Woodhead steam, much of it hitherto unseen, with not a Bo+Bo or Co-Co in sight, though readers will, perforce, have to tolerate the odd yard or two of contact wire here and there!

Ever since the first part of the trilogy appeared new aspects of history have emerged and further discoveries of photographic material have come to light. Much of this has languished unseen and has been waiting for a wider audience, thus enabling the appearance of this, perhaps the first book devoted entirely to "Steam over Woodhead".

Despite closure, now over thirty years ago, the Woodhead line retains an iconic status in the minds of enthusiasts. Indeed, two more books on the subject have appeared since the last one of my own and further appear to be in the pipeline.

Notwithstanding all this material, may I express the hope that this offering will forge another link in the Woodhead chain and provide an extra and useful addition to the history of this celebrated and most lamented section of railway.

E.M.Johnson,
Burnage,
Manchester.

June 2013

**Manchester London Road, April 10th 1945:** Smoke-blackened and war-weary, this was the station remembered by a generation that rejoice now in the title of "Silver Surfers." Before glancing up to the main station it is worth mentioning that the building to the left of the station approach was the LNWR goods warehouse, then re-branded as "LONDON MIDLAND AND SCOTTISH RAILWAY COMPANY'S GOODS STATION." Today is a Tuesday, the time is 3.43 pm – but too early yet for the office and shop workers who will soon be milling up the approach on their way home. Back then the Daily Dispatch was the newspaper of choice, while Golden Shred marmalade and Kolynos toothpaste were recommended appendages to daily life. For Mancunians bearing up after almost six years of war, the Stockport Bedding Co.Ltd. sold just the thing. To the right, along London Road itself, trolleybuses forming the 210 service to Hyde (Gee Cross) hum beneath the wires. The tower prominent on the right belongs to the London Road fire station on the corner of Whitworth Street. Glancing back to the station, a handcart loaded with sacks and boxes trundles up the cobbled way. Ahead, smoke trails from a sleeve-valved Daimler, possibly a taxi while more cabs cluster under the LMS' side of the verandah. Across on the LNER's side the cream and red outline of an MCTD bus makes its distinctive mark. In another thirteen years the winds of change will start to blow.

*Manchester City Engineers' Archive*

# INTRODUCTION

It might seem almost trite to mention that Manchester was in the forefront of railway development, something sealed by the opening of the Liverpool and Manchester Railway in September 1830. Very soon afterwards it became possible to make a railway journey from Manchester to London, albeit a very tedious one involving a circuitous deviation via Warrington and through industrialised Birmingham.

A mere year later, in 1831, an Act had been obtained for the construction of a railway between Manchester and Sheffield. This resulted in the formation of the Sheffield and Manchester Railway. A Parliamentary Bill received Royal Assent in August 1831 and capital was fixed at £530,000 with further borrowing power limited to the sum of a maximum of £176,000.

None other than the redoubtable George Stephenson had set out a proposal for a route that would have seen the new line start from Water Street, close to the Liverpool and Manchester terminus, before proceeding to Stockport. From here the great man proposed an alignment through the Goyt Valley then via Whaley Bridge and Chapel Milton towards the Hope Valley. Thus was anticipated, in small measure, the Midland's route to Sheffield – the Dore & Chinley Railway – of 1893. However, the great man's scheme was flawed: the use of inclined planes and a somewhat zany idea of using loaded limestone wagons to counterbalance loaded passenger trains ensured the demise of Stephenson's scheme.

It was left to Henry Sanderson, a Sheffield man, land surveyor and champion of rail travel between Sheffield and Manchester, to outline a route that, more or less, became the established alignment of what would become "the Woodhead Line". The services of Charles Vignoles, a prominent civil engineer, and Joseph Locke, Engineer of the Grand Junction Railway, were procured and the line's future was sealed by the deposition of a Bill to Parliament lodged in November 1836. Little opposition ensued; the only compromise being that the company would have to share the ¾ of a mile or so of line from Ardwick Junction into Manchester with the Manchester and Birmingham Railway. Thus was established the Sheffield, Ashton-under-Lyne and Manchester Railway – SAuL&M.

But, despite Stephenson's dismissal, plenty of obstacles remained to daunt the engineers of the new route. At Dinting and Mottram, hamlets both in the wild Derbyshire countryside, two large river valleys had to be conquered by the construction of stone and wooden viaducts. Worse still, some eight miles further east, beyond the sheltered calm of the Longdendale Valley, arose the need to bore a three-mile tunnel through the millstone grit of the Pennines. The Woodhead Tunnel, becoming one of three to bear the name, became synonymous with this, the first railway between Manchester and Sheffield. However, this single-bore tunnel at Woodhead soon proved inadequate for the growing traffic and a second bore was driven, opening on February 2nd 1852.

Steam, the modus operandi of the Victorian industrial machine, was, of course, the prime mover over the fledgling line. To a generation of enthusiasts weaned on the sight of Flying Scotsman, Mallard, Tornado and even Thomas the Tank, the early Sharp 2-2-2s of the SAuL&M must appear as something akin to a fantasy machine out of a science fiction novel. But "The Sharpies" did the business succeeded in turn by products from a host of contractors: Fenton Craven, Stephenson, Tulk & Ley and Wilson et al. In July 1846 the SAuL&M had become incorporated as the Manchester, Sheffield & Lincolnshire Railway (MS&L) The establishment of Gorton Works and production of its first locomotive in 1858 saw the beginning of what might be described as "in house" production of locomotives. Richard Peacock had been "Engine Driver No.1" and then first Locomotive Superintendent of the SAuL&M. After Peacock had joined forces with Charles Beyer to form the company of Beyer, Peacock & Co., the MS&L appointed William Grindley Craig to the post. Craig's tenure lasted but a year before he was succeeded by Charles Reboul Sacré, a personage recommended by Sturrock of the Great Northern Railway.

Due no doubt to the invention of photography, it is perhaps with the engines from the Sacré era (1859-1886) that begin to form the locomotive kaleidoscope that is readily recognisable to the student of Woodhead motive power. Sacré's engines exhibited grace and a degree of beauty. It is significant that he was aided during his period at Gorton by none other than S.W.Johnson who reigned on the Midland from 1876 to 1903, producing throughout his tenure a succession of most graceful and beautiful-looking railway engines. After Sacré came Parker then Pollitt; the latter forming something of an interregnum of a bare six years before the arrival of John George Robinson in 1900. Robinson's appointment and tenure coincided roughly with the appointment by the GCR board of Sam Fay as the company's General Manager. Both Robinson and Fay quickly set their marks and took the GCR from the end of the Victorian era, through the high-water mark of railways in the Edwardian period, the traumas of the First War and into the Grouping of 1923 that saw the Great Central subsumed into the LNER. It would be left to Sir Nigel Gresley and his successor, Edward Thompson, to produce the locomotives that followed the Gorton alumnae: all part of the motive power that became "Steam over Woodhead."

**Manchester London Road, September 1959:** Messrs.Connell & Finnigan's men survey the scene as demolition tackle rips in to demolish the 1866 station frontage and offices. The former GCR side stands defiantly behind the scaffolding tower. It was in these rooms that was planned the MS&L's London Extension along with all other aspects of boardroom life. This three-storey building would remain whilst, on the LNW side, a nine-storey glass and concrete edifice would be erected. To the left can be seen two hips of the roof of the former GCR grain and flour warehouse; the lettering reads: "BRITISH RAILWAYS FLOUR WAREHOUSE". Beyond stands the GCR London Warehouse – still with us today but now transformed into luxury apartments known as *The Place*. Imagine the same scene today: site fenced off with wire mesh and no one allowed anywhere near what was essentially dangerous work. Just in front can be glimpsed the two-storey wood and glass building that served temporarily for enquiries, seat and sleeper reservations, ladies waiting room and gents' hairdressing. The show went on, dangers notwithstanding.

*British Railways*

## MANCHESTER LONDON ROAD

From around 1958 the station fondly remembered as "Manchester London Road" began to change its identity. Scheduled to be demolished in its entirety, albeit in stages, was the station frontage – the vast Victorian swathe of brick and masonry - a building that had once housed the boardroom and headquarters of the MS&L before the company became the Great Central and moved south to Marylebone. Re-branded as "Manchester Piccadilly" from September $12^{th}$ 1960, the quintessential 1960s architecture of the station concourse lasted until 2000. Over the next two years another mighty re-fashioning of the frontage took place. Costing £27.9M and completed just in time for the opening of the XVII Commonwealth Games held in Manchester from July $25^{th}$ 2002, Piccadilly station now had a brand new, state-of-the-art almost arena-like concourse. It was a fitting prelude to the $21^{st}$ century, the third century in which the station had existed.

But to return, briefly, to origins: Train services over the Woodhead line commenced in stages. The very first passenger working saw life on Thursday November $11^{th}$ when a trial trip was made between Godley Toll Bar and Manchester. On board were the Chairman, Locke and the Directors The following week, with little or no fuss, the first public train was waved off from Godley on Wednesday, November $17^{th}$ at 8.00 am; the corresponding train left Manchester at 8.47 am. Fares from Manchester to Godley are recorded as being 1/6d, 1/2d & 10d (single fare – $1^{st}$/$2^{nd}$ & $3^{rd}$ class respectively). Passenger services to Sheffield began with due ceremony on December $22^{nd}$ 1845 (goods services to Glossop had begun on June 9th that year).

It must not be overlooked that Woodhead line services were as much about freight, especially coal, as anything else. At London Road the MS&L built an extensive goods warehouse. six storeys high it was known as "The London Warehouse" and fronted on to Ducie Street – the thoroughfare that runs across the bottom of the station approach. No exact date has come to light confirming when the London Warehouse was opened. However, an 1840s painting by Arthur Fitzwilliam Tait shows the building in situ, something that helps to confirm the matter. MS&L goods facilities were enhanced by a fruit and vegetable warehouse next door, along Ducie Street and a large grain and flour warehouse immediately behind the London building. Here, alongside the station approach was the goods warehouse of the LNWR. That company's goods facilities extended right into the station undercroft and over to Travis Street. Around here and along Sheffield Street were stabling facilities for the large number of horses that were employed in cartage operations. Amazingly, one could still see these splendid beasts at work around London Road in the early 1950s!

Services from Manchester used at first a station adjacent to Store Street. This was a puny affair with a mere two platforms: one for arrivals, the other for departures with six tracks between. A joint affair of course, the offices for the SAuL&M sat side by side with those of the M&B on the departure platform.
First known as "Bank Top", the name "London Road" was applied in 1847. Between 1865 and 1866 there was constructed on the station's north-east side the first two trainsheds with their distinctive elliptical roofs that became London Road's hallmark and are still with us today. A further extension on the south side, using the same pattern of roof and supporting cast-iron columns, was executed by the LNWR between 1880-1881. The MS&L extended their operations a year later when the company opened an additional platform on their own side.

The enlarged station was very much a joint affair with separate facilities and staffing, from stationmaster and goods managers downwards, a practice lasting into modern times. Much animosity had existed between the Sheffield and North-Western companies The MS&L's three platforms were distinguished by letters "A, B & C"; those of the LNWR were numbered from 1-12. For many years there was no platform 2 at London Road, something brought about by an intended re-modelling by the LNWR which never materialised. It was not until the rebuilding of 1958-60 for the Manchester-Crewe 25kV electrification scheme that a wholly logical platform numbering was instituted. Users of today's Manchester Piccadilly can still see the boundary between the 1865 and the 1881 stations when they enter the island platform that is numbered 8 and 9.

London Road's final extension took place in August 1910 when an additional station known as "Mayfield" was opened on the stations south side across Fairfield Street. A substantial red-brick affair with five platforms, Mayfield remained open to passengers until August 1960 after which it was used as a parcels concentration depot. Final closure was effected in 1986. Suggestions that the Mayfield site might be used for some sort of government offices have come to naught. This was followed by a plan under the "Manchester Hub" development scheme of the intention to build two further platforms on the south side of Piccadilly's platforms 13 and 14. Early this year (2013) a decision was made that Mayfield's roof was unsafe and demolition would be required. With the recent confirmation that HS2 will, eventually, reach Manchester a wholesale re-development of the Piccadilly station area would seem likely. Clearly, there are interesting times ahead.

**Manchester London Road, 1887:** No.561, a product of Kitson & Co., stands proudly outside the station. This locomotive, seen resplendent in exhibition finish* – two-tone lined green livery, polished brass and iron work, - had a curious origin. It seems that Messrs.Kitson wanted to exhibit a 4-4-0 loco for the Manchester Industrial Exhibition of 1887 held at White City, Old Trafford. However, the MS&L, likewise, wished to exhibit an engine and chose No.79, a member of Thomas Parker's Class 6D 2-4-0. A compromise was effected by Kitsons sending No.561which would ***(continued on page 6.....)***

*continued from p.6.........*
subsequently enter service for the MS&L becoming Class 2. Parker subsequently developed the design by building a further 30 engines with detail differences and these became Class 2A (LNE D7). No.561 and her sisters were used on the joint MS&L/GNR Manchester-King's Cross expresses as far as Grantham. Often overlooked by historians, these workings dated back to 1857 and lasted until the 1920s. The 2A 4-4-0s were used as well on services in South Yorkshire and Lincolnshire. No.561 was withdrawn as LNER No.5561 in September 1928. The 6-wheeled 1st/3rd oil-lit stock in the background belongs, too, to the MS&L and was used on the local services to Glossop and Hadfield; it was still around in the 1930s! Signalling buffs should note the two LNWR slotted-post signals controlling operations on the company's goods lines behind. Produced at Crewe from 1874 they formed a marked contrast to the later distinctive squat pattern of semaphores of the early 20th century.

**The actual condition for the 1887 exhibition differed slightly from that seen here.* *Author's collection*

**(Right)** Valour's nameplate, seen at Gorton Works c.1955. The plate was mounted on the corner of the Iron Foundry facing the main works entrance.

**Manchester London Road, 1921:** The 4-6-0 type reached its apotheosis on the GCR with Robinson's six "Lord Faringdon" Class 9P engines. Completed at Gorton between 1917 and 1920, the sextet exuded grace and power in equal measure. Storming away from platform "A" is No.1165 *Valour* with an express for Marylebone. *Valour* is seen in this photograph equipped for oil-burning, a conversion carried out to alleviate coal shortages during the protracted miners' strike of that year. Robinson's "Unolco" system had been applied to two of the class, but the conversion was brief, lasting a mere two months. The immaculate condition presented by *Valour*, is a reflection of the esteem and pride in which this, the Great Central's tribute to the company's war dead, was held at its home shed of Gorton. Yearly, on Armistice Day, November 11th, the engine was always specially groomed to carry out its memorial duty. This consisted of hauling the 8.20 morning train to Sheffield conveying men and their families to the Armistice service at Victoria station where the GC had erected memorial plaques. When No.1165 was withdrawn in December 1947 it was strongly rumoured that the loco was to be preserved. In the event, only the nameplates survived and one of these was subsequently stolen from its memorial plinth outside St.Barnabas' church, Rolling stock enthusiasts should note the 4-wheeled van alongside *Valour*: a 5-ton milk and fruit van, it was one of six built at Gorton in 1898. *H.S.T.Parrish*

**Manchester London Road, 1913:** No.423, *Sir Sam Fay*, the pioneer of Robinson's impressive Class 1 4-6-0 awaits departure from the GC's "A" platform with an express for London Marylebone. Much publicity accompanied the launch of the new locomotive, something doubtless down to its namesake. No.423 was completed at Gorton on December 14th 1912; a further five engines, named after cities served by the GCR appeared in the first few months of 1913. History has not been kind to the "Sir Sams" or "Cities" as they were variously known. However, they appeared competent on the duties they were assigned and found favour with the loco crews that handled them. In his definitive biography of J.G.Robinson, David Jackson records that in 1913 No.423 was deployed on the 10.00 am express from London Road to Marylebone in the charge of driver A.Kenworthy.

*P.F.Cooke*

**Manchester London Road, c.1904**: Striding away from platform "A" is Robinson Atlantic No.192 at the head of an express for Marylebone. Built by Beyer, Peacock & Co. and completed in December 1903, this was the first of Robinson's handsome 4-4-2 tender engines held by many to be some of the most handsome locomotives of the Edwardian era. Popularly known as "Jersey Lillies", though the origin of the sobriquet is uncertain, the Atlantics were among the most successful of Robinson's designs. Of particular interest is the appearance of the coaching stock: liveried à la GWR with cream upper panels offset against the chocolate lower ones; this had displaced an earlier scheme with grey upper panels. In the background, again, note the LNWR slotted-post signal and the hydraulic lift to convey wagons and vans "downstairs" to the goods yard on Travis Street. The summit at Woodhead will be some forty minutes away, the journey time to Marylebone was around a little under four and a half hours within this period. *P.F.Cooke*

**Manchester London Road, April 25th 1957:** Both the GCR and the LNW modernised the signalling arrangements at London Road in the first decade of the twentieth century. A.F.Bound the company's brilliant young Signal Superintendent had studied American practice and had adopted a pneumatically-operated system by the British Pneumatic Company for points and signals along the busy stretch as far as Newton, near Hyde. London Road's GCR box (commissioned in 1909) had 82 slides; these appear in a neat row beneath the signal and point indicating lights and track circuit diagram. All set above polished mahogany cabinets, the whole looking as Edwardian and dependable as the GCR itself. *Not* of Edwardian origin are the brown earthenware teapot and accompanying mug; but what aspect of railway operation could function satisfactorily without these indispensible accoutrements?! The British Power Company's system served the line well; conversion to electro-pneumatic operation did not come about until the early 1930s.

*Dr.J.W.F.Scrimgeour/*
*Signalling Record Society*

**Manchester London Road, Ducie Street Goods Depot, Summer 1921:** To the sheer and utter frustration of railway historians, pictures of workings in and out of goods depots are very few and far between. Doubtless, photographers were hampered by security considerations, or was it just preference for passenger locomotives and trains that has bequeathed us this paucity? Hard on the heels of the Class 1 "Sir Sam Fay" 4-6-0s came the smaller-wheeled, 5ft.7in. version – the "Glenalmonds" - turned out from Gorton between 1913-15. The class was designed for working express goods and fish trains, the latter a speciality of the GCR with the company's presence at the fishing ports of Grimsby and Hull. No.443 is seen awaiting departure from Ducie Street with a mixed freight. The engine is fitted with Robinson's "Unolco" system of oil-burning, apparatus carried from June to October 1921. The loco stands on the bridge carrying the tracks of the goods warehouse over Sheffield Street and Boad Street; the GC's grain and flour warehouse stands behind. Just beyond the train's brake van can be glimpsed the station's LNWR's warehouses. No.443 was withdrawn in March 1948. The Ducie Street warehouses were closed in 1965. "Gateway House" and the Piccadilly station car park now cover the land today. *P.F.Cooke*

**Manchester London Road, c.1880s:** What locomotive enthusiast could resist the sight of this charming little 0-6-0 saddle tank engine? No.407 was an 1873 product of Manning Wardle and was bought in 1876 by the MS&L for £2,800 from Messrs.Logan & Hemmingway, civil engineering contractors who were engaged by the MS&L on various projects. One of a pair of locos that became Class 4 in the company's engine list, No.407 had 3ft.9in coupled wheels and cylinders sized 14in X 20in. Worthy of mention are the wooden brake blocks – screw operated, brass steam collector over the firebox and simple weatherboard cab, inside of which were housed twin Salter safety valves! Engaged at London Road on shunting work in the Ducie Street yards, the little charmer would doubtless never have ventured much further east than Gorton. Behind the low wall can be seen the roofs of houses along the cluster of the mean little streets – such as Baines Place, Scott Street and Walter Street, all surrounding London Road over a hundred and thirty years ago. The hipped roof behind the engine is a hydraulic accumulator tower powering the hoists for the LNW goods yards off Travis Street and Sheffield Street. *Author's collection*

**Manchester London Road, c.1925:** In the early post-Grouping years the Robinson Atlantics were still doing capable express work over the GCR's London Extension. Working largely to and from Leicester; the latter shed deploying no less than seventeen of these fine machines. One such was No.5266 seen here leaving London Road on more mundane duties – a Manchester to Glossop and Hadfield local comprised of the usual rake of 6-wheelers (first coach numbered 395). The loco is wearing the second period LNER livery of Apple green lined black and white, something doubtless applied after a recent overhaul at Gorton – hence its appearance on humble running-in duties before working back south. *P.F.Cooke*

**Manchester London Road, c.1919-22:** This splendid study shows former MS&L 2-4-2 tank Class 3 No.599 outside the station, close to London Road's No.2 signalbox; Mayfield station can be seen clearly in the background. Local train workings from Manchester over GCR lines served towns and villages over a wide area, for example: Fairfield, Guide Bridge, Hayfield, New Mills, Stalybridge, Macclesfield and Glossop and as far east as Hadfield in Derbyshire. In due course all the Class 3s received Belpaire boilers, No.599 carrying hers from May 1914 which helps to date the photograph. This picture (and that above) is from the camera of P.F.Cooke, an enigmatic character who lived in Huddersfield and photographed extensively in the Manchester area within this period. *P.F.Cooke*

3rd-SINGLE SINGLE-3rd
Manchester (London Road) to
Manch'ter (Lon. Rd.) Manch'ter (Lon. Rd.)
Ashburys Ashburys
ASHBURYS
(M) 0/4 FARE 0/4 (M)
FOR CONDITIONS SEE OVER

**Manchester London Road, April 12th 1933:** Taken from the GC signalbox where the clock should be showing around 1.34, D11 "Director" No.5509 *Prince Albert* heads into the terminus with the 8.45 am Down express from Marylebone. Spot the LNWR 4-4-0 leaving on the LMS side and the copious amount of freight traffic. Notice, too, the densely-packed terrace houses, the chimneys, mill building and surrounding murk. All typical of the industrial Manchester within this period.
*R.D.Pollard/Manchester Loco Society*

**Manchester London Road, July 5th 1933:** At the same position as the picture above, but this time at ground-level, the 8.45 Down Restaurant Car express from Marylebone runs into London Road hauled by B7 No.5477 providing a marked (and untypical) contrast to the shot of the "Director." The LMS' London Road No.2 signalbox sits erect to the right with No.1, sometimes known as "Chapelfield", seen faintly in the distance.
*R.D.Pollard/Manchester Loco Society*

**Manchester London Road, August 7th 1933:** A first look at the B17s, or "Sandringhams", the handsome Gresley/North British 4-6-0s that began to make their mark on services over Woodhead from 1928. With the lined Apple green livery polished to perfection and shining in the afternoon sun, No.2834 *Hinchinbrooke* pulls briskly away from platform "A" with the 3.50 pm express for Marylebone. By the looks of things the tender's nominal coal capacity of 4 tons has been somewhat exceeded with the coal piled up to the limits of the loading gauge. It was, after all, 206 miles to London!

*R.D.Pollard/Manchester Loco Society*

**Manchester London Road, August 1952:** Though the purist might argue that the C13 4-4-2 tanks were never seen over Woodhead at the head of a train, the ubiquitous engines were both long-lived and useful specimens earning their keep on the GC system for over half a century. In the early 1950s the Gorton C13s were working in and out of London Road on the Glossop and Hadfield locals as well as over at Guide Bridge on the Oldham and Stalybridge trains. In and around the station itself the tanks did sterling duty as empty carriage pilots. On such a duty No.67439 has ventured over onto "foreign" territory – the former LMS side of the station. Looking immaculate, the loco has just emerged from Gorton works after a general overhaul. Notice the usual gaggle of spotters dotted around; the loco is even receiving the attention of a lady stood on the MSJ&A platform! Over at platform 1 an ex-LMS "Crab" No.42776 awaits departure with an express.

*David Green collection*

**Manchester London Road, August 8th 1935:** A "Sam" in LNER days: Barking out of "A" platform is (by then) Class B1 4-6-0 No.5427 *City of London* with the 12.40pm (SO) express to Cleethorpes carrying through coaches for Hull. The term "Express" in reality applied only to the part of the journey between Manchester and Sheffield. For as well as the usual stop at Guide Bridge, the 12.40 paid calls at Dunford Bridge, Penistone, Deepcar and Oughty Bridge before arriving in Sheffield Victoria at 1.52. Six minutes were allowed here for the Hull portion to be detached. After Sheffield the train became "all stations to Cleethorpes" following the old MS&L route via Worksop, Retford, Gainsborough and Barnetby, stopping everywhere en route to arrive at the famous East Coast seaside resort at 4.42. One can only hope the sun was shining and the tide was out! *R.D.Pollard/Manchester Loco Society*

*cont.from page 14.........*

**Manchester London Road, Summer 1939:** War clouds were looming on the horizon when Kenneth Oldham snatched this shot of A1 No.4478 *Hermit* waiting alongside platform "A" at the head of the 2.20 pm express to London Marylebone. Alongside, on "B" platform, a GC 4-4-2 tank awaits departure with a local train. Gresley A1 Pacifics had first visited Gorton in the early post-Grouping years for running-in work, typically from Manchester Central on locals to Chester. (What a contrast to today's "Nodding Donkeys" on the same services!) It was in 1938 that A1s returned to Manchester, this time to work the Marylebone expresses out of London Road over Woodhead. No.2558 *Tracery* arrived first, in September 1938, this was followed by No.4474 *Victor Wild* and No.4478 *Hermit* – both in March 1939, No.4473 *Solario* followed in May. The last of this Manchester quintet was No.2554 *Woolwinder,* arriving in August 1939. As the war proceeded more Pacifics were drafted in with fourteen being allocated, though largely short-term, during the war years. Longer-term Pacific working did not return to the GC section until 1949. Moving then into the BR era, A3s were based at Leicester and Neasden, working over Woodhead in and out of London Road until the arrival of electric traction in 1954. *Kenneth Oldham MBE*

**Manchester London Road, June 20th 1948:** The alien-looking bulk of GWR No.6990 *Witherslack Hall* bears down on the photographer as it enters the station with the 11-coach 10.00 am express from Marylebone. The occasion was, of course, the interchange loco trials making June 1948 an exciting time for Manchester enthusiasts. *Witherslack Hall* was trialled over the GC main line along with LMS "Black 5" No.5253 and SR Bulleid Pacific No.34006 *Bude*. (The Up working was the 8.25 am from London Road). Contemporary accounts would appear to favour the Bulleid engine in respect of timekeeping. Meanwhile, over on former Midland lines, working out of Manchester Central on expresses to St.Pancras, another Bulleid machine, No.21C105 *Barnstaple,* could be seen along with LNER Thompson B1 No.61251 *Oliver Bury.* And for those enthusiasts with a penchant for more modern motive power, the newly-built LMS diesel No.10000 was growling its way in and out of Manchester Central with the St.Pancras expresses. Happily, *Witherslack Hall* is still with us today and there is even a project afoot to build a replica of one of the pioneer LMS diesels. *R.D.Pollard/Manchester Loco Society*

**Manchester London Road, c.1950-51:** What, the reader may well ask, is a Cambridge engine doing at London Road? Although the Gresley B17s had been regular visitors to Manchester from 1928 on the through workings to and from Harwich and later on the Marylebone expresses, the engines' through cross-country duties are thought to have ended with the cessation of lodging turns from 1942. Gorton Works did much shopping work on B17s pre-war and this practice continued from the end of 1949 until the middle of 1953 when the works carried out the bulk of the repairs on the 4-6-0s. Indeed, within this period, no less than 63 of the original 73 B17s (but excluding the B2 rebuilds) visited Gorton for work listed as being between "non-classified" and "general" repairs. In this (undated) photo No.61636 *Harlaxton Manor* is seen at London Road having backed down into the station and awaiting departure with a local train. 61636 paid five visits to Gorton within the period stated: three were in 1950, two in 1951 - the loco was allocated to Cambridge from 4/6/1950 to 19/1/52. While the fireman trims the coal a young boy is having the time of his life peering into the cab. An embryo engine driver maybe? Happy days! *I.Hatton/courtesy Irwell Press*

**Manchester London Road, April 4th 1953:** This fine study of V2 No.60831 must be amongst the last pictures of steam on the former GCR/LNER side of the station before preparations for electrification began. Unsullied by any presence of the OHL the loco prepares to move off in charge of the 2.10 pm express for Marylebone. V2s were first seen over Woodhead in 1938 when No.4798 (BR 60827) was drafted to Gorton to work the Marylebone trains in partnership with A1 No.2558 *Tracery*. The building at the end "A" platform was a shunters' cabin and features on many photographs taken in the vicinity. Notice the GCR-pattern shunting signal in the background together with the floodlight, both signs of the one-time high level of freight operations, largely unsung and unseen that existed here for around 120 years.
*B.K.B.Green*

**Between London Road and Ardwick Junction, c.1952:** K3 No.61980 storms along the Up (Eastern Region) line towards Ardwick Junction with an eight coach express. The K3s were late-comers to the Woodhead line, not arriving until towards the end of 1935. 61980 was allocated to Gorton from March 4th 1937, though she was based at Annesley throughout the 1950s. The tracks between London road and Ardwick were very much "two-company" territory back then. Just beyond the K3 a cast-iron plate fastened to a sleeper end read: **"LMR MAINTENANCE ENDS ER - MAINTENANCE BEGINS"** leaving no doubt as to where responsibility lay! Seen in the background to the right of the train is a reminder of days gone by: the ecclesiastical-looking building with the small tower is the Chancery Lane Sunday School. Dating from 1880, the building replaced two earlier schools: one on Bank Meadow and another on Chancery Lane itself.
*Arthur Bendell/courtesy of J.Wells*

**Ardwick, August 16th 1951:** The B7s have been thinned out and are almost history over former Great Central routes now. Representing the new order of motive power over Woodhead is Thompson B1 4-6-0 No.61247 *Lord Burghley* seen rounding the curve at Ardwick with an Up express. 61247 was built by the North British Loco.Co. and entered traffic in October 1947. Framing the picture is a handsome bracket semaphore signal, one installed as part of A.F.Bound's re-signalling programme in the early 1900s and referred to earlier. Off to the right, standing on a low viaduct, is the L&Y's short branch - "The Lanky Branch" - of 1848 to Miles Platting via Midland Junction and Philips Park. Behind the viaduct carrying the branch can be seen some of the terraced houses that so characterised this area over seventy years ago: behind Higher Sheffield Street - which paralleled the railway - lay the "Royal" streets: King Street, Queen Street and Princess Street fringed by Midland Street and Tempest Street. Behind these rows of humble dwellings spot the chimneyed edifice that was Chester's Brewery providing employment for generations of Ardwick locals and whose products must have quenched many a thirst in the Albert Inn, the Clock Face, the Hare and Hounds, the Marsland Hotel and the Star Inn. The characters sat on the platform seat are probably workers from the nearby Ardwick carriage sheds sited just beyond the Up platform. Dominating the background is the tower of St.Andrew's church, Ancoats; a familiar landmark, one often seen on pictures taken on the London Road station approaches, but seldom referred to. Long gone today, alas. Across on the south-west side of the former LNW tracks is Ardwick Junction signalbox. Qualifying as one of the loftiest boxes in the Manchester area it actually stood on Temperance Street, well below the level of the viaduct. *Neville Fields/Manchester Loco Society*

**Ardwick, July 10th 1948:** Looking grimy and woebegone is B7 No.E1380 slogging round the curve at Ardwick with an Up local train. As GCR 472, the loco had emerged new from Gorton in the summer of 1922. Withdrawal of the B7s had begun in April 1948 and all had gone by the Spring of 1950. Ardwick station was served on the down side by an island platform; a connecting lattice footbridge, seen behind the train, led to the up platform. A fashionable suburb of Manchester in Victorian days, Ardwick had become somewhat industrialised and run-down by the post-war era. The long single-storey building standing off to the right was a carriage shed serving the LNER's side of London Road, again - one of many signs that this section of railway was very much a "two-company" affair.

*NevilleFields/ManchesterLocoSociety*

**Ardwick, July 10th 1948:** Rounding the curve through the station with an Up express is North British Loco Co's B1 No.61316 resplendent in freshly minted LNER Apple green, lined black and white. Adorned by plain "BRITISH RAILWAYS" on the tender side, the loco, then barely two months into traffic, was one of the sixty-six B1s built by NB which first saw service under the new regime. *Neville Fields/Manchester Loco Society*

**Ardwick, looking east to Ashburys, 1951:** An aspect rarely seen by the camera: the station's two platforms were of a staggered nature. The up platform (seen in the B7 picture) was a short way back towards Manchester, while that on the Down side was an island: Down main on one side, a down passenger loop on the other. Coming along the Down main is B1 61155 with an express, probably a Marylebone train. One of fifty B1s built by Vulcan Foundry in 1947 the loco was one of eight allocated to Gorton, each with its own driver. "1155" being the 'property' at this time of driver Dick Ball. A second (unidentified) B1 waits to exit the carriage sidings. Beyond these were extensive goods sidings developed with the quadrupling of the line and controlled by Ardwick No.3 signalbox. George Simms' map of the Manchester railways dated 1858 shows just two siding roads here alongside the Up line as being owned by the Great Northern Railway. Spread out to the right is the yard belonging to Manchester Corporation's Hyde Road bus garage. Extending through the viaduct carrying the ex-LNW line the area was known as "The Permanent Way". Used then for storing buses - in the (now) quaint-looking livery of red and cream, the 12-acre site had once been the home of Manchester City FC. The multi-storey building in the left background was Heywood House, one of the ghastly post-war housing developments in this part of the city. Standing proud in the rear is the rather splendid-looking St.Benedict's church on Bennett Street. This fine building survives today as the home of the Manchester Climbing Centre. *Geoff Parrish*

**Ashburys West Junction, June 18th 1948:** Seen two days before *Witherslack Hall* was photographed on a return working, here is another one of the protagonists in the celebrated exchange trials over the Manchester-Marylebone route. LMS "Black 5" No.45253 approaches Ashburys at the head of the 8.25 am express from London Road to Marylebone; note the dynamometer car behind the tender. The bridge in the foreground spans Gorton Road; Ashburys West box peeps out on the left-hand side. *Harold.D.Bowtell/Manchester Loco Society*

## ASHBURYS (FOR BELLE VUE)

The Ashbury Company, or more correctly "The Ashbury Railway Carriage & Iron Company Ltd.", of carriage and wagon building fame, gave their name to the station adjoining their premises. These were bounded by Pottery Lane, Ashton Lane (Ashton Old Road in modern times), the GCR main line and Gorton Lane in the Ardwick district of East Manchester. John Ashbury had founded his business in Knott Mill, Manchester in 1837 before moving, finally, to Ashton Old Road, Openshaw in 1846. Ashburys station came later, opening in July 1855. John Ashbury had been given land of an area comprising just over one acre for part of his carriage works by the MS&L. As a quid pro quo Ashbury would hand to the MS&L a strip of land on the north side of the railway some 175 yards long west of Pottery Lane. An agreement dated December 31st 1864 stating clearly: "for widening the company's railway." Ashburys flourished as a concern producing not only rolling stock, but associated components such as turntables, cranes, bridge components and sundry ironwork. In 1902 Ashburys merged with the Metropolitan Carriage & Wagon Company of Birmingham and from 1903 the company became a component supplier to the Metropolitan Amalgamated Group. In 1928 the former Ashburys works closed completely. On June 15th 1931 the LNER opened a goods depot on the site known as "Ardwick East"; the depot lasting well into BR days. Although the exact date of closure has not been determined, Ardwick East was still in use as a depot for Rail Express Parcels as late as 1979. In 2012 the site was cleared to make way for the new regional operating centre which will ultimately take control of signalling and telecommunications encompassing the whole of the north-west.

References in railway history almost always favour the MS&L/GCR when referring to Ashburys and its environs. (Incidentally, the apostrophe in the station's title was dropped long before Lynne Truss published her famous "Eats, Shoots and Leaves.") However, the Midland Railway, too, had considerable presence in this part of Manchester. The company possessed extensive coal, goods and cattle-handling facilities hereabouts as well as wagon repair shops on the north side of the MS&L's yards at Ardwick. Midland territory began west of Ashburys station at Ashburys West Junction ("Midland Goods Junction" prior to 1889). The junction served the company's Ancoats goods warehouse of 1870 via the Ancoats Junction line which bisected the Midland and MS&L yards at Ardwick. At Midland Junction the line from Ashburys West was joined by the L&Y's branch up from Ardwick which continued along to Philips Park.

East of Ashburys station the Midland's line from Romiley Junction (Sheffield & Midland Joint of 1875) joined the MS&L's main line. This was Ashburys East Junction, one time plain "Ashburys Junction" before the opening of the Ancoats Junction line. An Act of Parliament dated 1888 was required to enable Midland trains coming off the Joint line at Ashburys East to traverse MS&L tracks for a mere 15 chains in order to access the line from Ashburys West. Just beyond Ashburys East Junction, on the north side of the main line, were the Ashburys goods yards always referred to by railwaymen as "Ashburys Bottom Yard" and "Ashburys Top Yard" respectively and once providing an important focal point for Woodhead freight traffic. In the fork between the MS&L's main line and the Sheffield & Midland Joint line was the Midland's Belle Vue engine shed. Known by the company as "Manchester" it opened in 1870; its passenger services were largely handed over to the joint shed at Trafford Park when this opened in 1895. Belle Vue engine shed closed in April 1956. Ashburys station survives into the 21st century, although the MS&L buildings were demolished in the 1980s to make way for the more functional and vandal-proof modern structures. Ashburys East signalbox, a hardy survivor from the Bound era was abolished on September 19th 2011, its function now controlled by a "Work Station" designated "Manchester East" and housed on the site of the former Edgeley loco shed at Stockport; the centre controls also the Stalybridge and Guide Bridge areas.

**Ashburys station, April 18th 1939:** Twilight of the MS&L 2-4-2 Tanks. Seen working a Manchester London Road to Marple train is F1 2-4-2 tank No.5732. Worthy of a mention is the rather fine GCR Clerestory coach behind the loco and the splendid bracket signal protecting Ashburys West Junction.

*Neville Fields/Manchester Loco Society*

**Ashburys station, August 18th 1951:** "ASHBURYS FOR BELLE VUE" reads the station's name board. Belle Vue, the once-popular leisure attraction developed by John Jennison from 1836, was served in its heyday by no less than four stations. Ashburys was by the most far-flung, being – even as the crow flies – over ¾ of a mile away. B1 No.61311 has travelled from Blackpool via Manchester Victoria, Miles Platting and Philips Park and is seen coming off the Ancoats Junction line at Ashburys West Junction. Beyond the platforms the train will turn off the GCR main line at Ashburys East Junction to take the Sheffield & Midland Joint line as far as Romiley Junction. From here 61311 will proceed through Marple and Strines to New Mills South Junction heading towards Chinley. At Chinley North Junction this Saturday train will follow the Midland's Dore & Chinley line of 1893 towards Sheffield and home. A fascinating deviation of just 15 chains from our "Steam Over Woodhead" theme. *Neville Fields/Manchester Loco Society*

**Ashburys, Pottery Lane, November 5th 1935:** A view of bridge No.6 – at 1 mile 51 chains from London Road taking the GCR's line over Pottery Lane; Ashburys station stands off to the left. The work in progress was the replacement of the original bridge spans with steel structures making a widened roadway in the process. The new spans were a product of Messrs. Fairfield of Chepstow and were not ready for rolling into place until May 21st 1936 – a long job! On the right-hand side was Garden Terrace where the Ford 15cwt/1 ton lorry – RJ 4022 - is parked, the property of H.Evers Ltd., General Contractors of Ancoats. Notice the group of small boys, fascinated, maybe by the sight of a large camera with the obligatory black cloth over the photographer's head! Beyond, on the corner of Ashton Old Road are the premises of Messrs.Crossley Brothers, manufacturers of oil and gas engines. One of three works in the area, it was here that Crossleys began to manufacture the renowned Otto gas engines in the early 1870s. *LNER/British Railways*

**Ashburys East Junction, c.1936:** B17s first appeared in Manchester in 1928 when No.2802 *Walsingham* arrived On November 30th to work the Harwich Boat train, a service unofficially dubbed as "The North Country Continental." (qv) No.2840 *Somerleyton Hall* had been allocated to Gorton in early June1933 along with two other class members, Nos.2841 & 2842. Then, as well as handing the boat trains, the new 4-6-0s were put to work on the London expresses, services handled latterly up to that point by "Directors". Gorton and Neasden shared ownership of *Somerleyton Hall* until the Autumn of 1938, which should help to date the photograph. In this view the loco is seen crossing Ashburys East Junction with an express from London Marylebone, possibly the 8.45 am departure. The Sheffield & Midland Joint line to Romiley veers off to the right, first stop – "Belle Vue".

*William Lees*

# GORTON TANK – WORKS AND SHED OF THE FORMER GCR

Gorton works and shed fits one of the numerous examples (at least as far as railway premises go) of a place name not fitting its true location, for the entire complex sat in neighbouring Openshaw. Despite this geographical anomaly, however, the "Gorton" tag remains the commonly accepted term for the works, so "Gorton" it remains. Known to generations of Manchester railwaymen and enthusiasts as "Gorton Tank", the origins of the name remained obscure until the recent discovery of a 19th-century press cutting containing a report from no less an authority than Richard Peacock. Speaking at an annual distribution of prizes at the Openshaw Mechanics Institution in 1883 Peacock recounted how, at the neighbouring Longsight works in the early years of the Manchester & Birmingham Railway a certain individual hit upon the idea of impregnating sleepers with creosote by means of hydraulic pressure within a large tank. After the process had been in use for some 18 months, the site became known as "Tank Yard" (Longsight shed until modern times was overlooked by a street known as "Tank Row"). When the M&B line opened, Longsight became the site of a small locomotive works which became known as "The Tank." In like manner, when the Lancashire & Yorkshire Railway opened their Miles Platting works this, too, had the "Tank" tag applied to it. By this time the "Tank" title was being applied quite widely to engineering works and was, in turn, adopted as a pseudonym for Gorton Works. So, the "Tank" handle stuck and became the generic term used by Mancunians and ex-pats the world over to describe the ex-GCR's works and shed complex. In its formative years the SAuL&M and the MS&L had relied on contractors for their motive power. Gorton's first locomotive emerged in March 1858. An 0-6-0 named Archimedes and numbered 6, it had 5ft. dia. coupled wheels and was designated Class 5.

Almost as well known as "The Tank" was "The Birdcage", the lattice girder footbridge that gave access to the shed and works from Wellington Street on the east side of the complex. Indeed East Manchester as a whole was choc-a-bloc with engineering and associated industries. Here, in Gorton and Openshaw rubbing shoulders in a space a little over a mile long, was once the Ashbury carriage works, referred to previously, the Otto gas engine works, the engineering works of Armstrong Whitworth, Gorton engine shed and, next door, the one-time locomotive, carriage and wagon works. The MS&L's facility had moved up to Openshaw as far back as 1858 (a smaller place had existed previously at Dog Lane in Dukinfield) at the behest of Richard Peacock, MS&L "Driver No.1".

Mention of the name Richard Peacock calls to mind another famous locomotive works: The Gorton Foundry aka Beyer, Peacock & Co. "Beyers", as they were always known to Mancunians, began life in 1854 in premises on the south side of the main line and directly opposite "The Tank". Peacock, a Yorkshireman, had defected from the MS&L to join forces with Charles Frederick Beyer and Henry Robertson, a Scotsman. Beyer was born in Saxony in 1813, a product of a humble background indeed. Locomotive production commenced in 1855 and the company went on to grow into one of the world's leading producers of railway locomotives. In 1908 they acquired the services of Herbert William Garratt who developed the articulated locomotive into almost an art form and making the name "Beyer Garratt" almost as famous as that of the founding company. The first Garratt was completed in 1909. Beyer, Peacock had a long association with both the GCR and built many locomotives for the company. The ties were underlined after Grouping with the company producing locomotives for the LNER. Relations with the ancien regime were further strengthened by Sir Sam Fay, the former GCR's General Manager, becoming Chairman of Peacocks and J.G.Robinson, the company's loco engineer, serving as a director.

Producing originally locomotives, carriages and wagons, the rolling stock side at Gorton was moved out to purpose-built premises at Dukinfield in 1910. Over the many years of its existence Gorton did much remarkable work. Little-known was the works' excellence in pattern-making and foundry work – cylinders were cast here for many Gresley designs, including the redoubtable A4s. Sir Nigel was a frequent visitor and had face-to-face dealings with one of the chargehand pattern-makers, Edward Hardwick.

Gorton had its own station (Gorton & Openshaw) "G and O" to many and two important junctions: one east, the other west of the station. West, and beyond the works and shed was Priory Junction where the shed and works were accessed off from the GC main line; east was Gorton Junction where a curve enabled traffic from "The Fallowfield Line" (Manchester Central Station Railway) to reach Manchester's London Road station via Hyde Road junction. Traversing the main line at the station's west end was the aqueduct (structure No.11) carrying the Stockport Branch (4 miles, 70 chains) of the Manchester & Ashton-under-Lyne canal running from Clayton down via Reddish to Heaton Norris, Stockport. Abandoned from 1963, the canal branch served a whole variety of industries: cotton spinning mills, iron and chemical works and coal wharves. The GCR possessed its own canal boat works at Gorton, aside from the loco, carriage and wagon works.

But for the outbreak of war in 1939 Gorton may well have diversified into electric loco maintenance, for it was intended that servicing of the locomotives for the MSW 1500V dc electrification should be carried out there. In the event, such facilities were established at Reddish on the Fallowfield line, just west of Hyde Road Junction. Building and repair of locomotives at Gorton continued up until May 1963. Soon afterwards the entire area was cleared and razed to the ground to become the site of Manchester's Smithfield produce market. Beyer, Peacock & Co. carried on as steam locomotive builders until 1958 after which the company diversified into the manufacture of diesel and electric traction. Two notable examples of the new motive power being the "Hymek" diesels and the ten Class 82 25kV locomotives produced in collaboration with Metropolitan Vickers, also of Manchester.

**Gorton, shed yard looking east, c.mid-1930s:** The industrial murk of East Manchester provides an appropriate atmosphere for this aerial view of the Gorton shed and works complex. Taken from the coaling tower, in the background can be seen five of the six hipped roofs of the erecting shops; the 24-road engine shed is out of sight off to the left. The twin-bunker mechanical coaler of 500-ton capacity and wet ash pits were part of some much-needed modernisation carried out here by the LNER in the early 1930s. Below the photographer a crane fills one of a line of wagons with waste ash from the pits in the centre. The ash pits, at 280 ft.long, were among the largest on the LNER system. Maintaining the ash pits was a 24-hour job and was supervised during the war years by W.Lord, W.Whitelaw, and S.Owen. Coaling and watering of locos were also the responsibility of these three foremen. Ash removal was a key job and a hitch in its smooth running could cause chaos in the shed yard. Emptying the pits took at least four hours and up to 24 wagons were needed for disposal. The wagons were moved to Ashburys "Bottom Yard" before disposal on the tip at Dinting. Moving to the yard below a number of GC locos stand, though the quality of the picture inhibits positive identification. Over to the left can be made out the line colloquially known as "The Cheshire Road" and "Runner Road" – connections that gave access to the Up and Down Slow lines. Gorton enginemen described traversing these as "going over the Alps". Across on the main line is Priory Junction; the signalbox controlling operations in and out of the yard from the main line can be clearly seen. Along here a GC "Director" 4-4-0, one of the earlier type – Class D10 - can be seen backing down towards London Road. In front of Priory Junction box the top part of the former Midland shed at Belle Vue is visible; ahead of the box, to the right of the main line stands the Gorton Foundry of Beyer, Peacock & Co.

*Author's collection*

**Gorton Works yard, c.mid-1930s:** A move down to ground-level takes us to the front of the erecting shops. An array of locomotives is seen: most are parted from their tenders and await their call forward into the works. Over to the right is B9 4-6-0 No.6105 (GC Class 8G of 1906 built by Beyer, Peacock); in front is a Robinson 2-8-0 followed by a 4-4-0 – possibly a D6. Moving to the left a little, two large domes suggest a pair of J10s, one boiler has had its clothing removed. Nearer to the camera the picture is much clearer; here is B8 (Class 1A) 4-6-0 No. 5004 *Glenalmond*; in front are a pair of 0-6-0s, possibly J9s or J10s with a tank engine heading the queue. Notice the lone figure squatting on the ground; out of sight of the foreman, maybe he was snatching an unofficial break? Beyond the "NE" wagons a final GC loco is seen, in steam this time, but not identifiable. Prominent in the foreground are two lots of cast driving wheel centres stored outside for "seasoning" and awaiting the application of some of the steel tyres seen stacked around in ample profusion. The wooden shed outside "3-Bay" was inhabited in latter days by a character known as "Arthur"; his domain was used for storing firebars and cotton waste used for raising steam for testing purposes *William Lees*

**Gorton shed yard, mid-1930s:** Turning around half-circle from our previous view of this area we look west across Priory Junction and down towards Ashburys. Dominating the yard is the coaling tower forever known as "The Cenotaph". Below, the scene buzzes with activity with three or four locos close to the coaler. Two former GC locos are clearly discernible: both are "Fish engines", GC Class 8 4-6-0s, now LNER B5. Below the camera is No.5183, while looking across and alongside "The Cheshire Road" can be seen No.6068. Through the smoky haze off to the right is the engineering works of Messrs.Armstrong Whitworth sited along (appropriately) Whitworth Street behind Ashton Old Road. *William Lees*

**Openshaw, Railway Hotel, July 4th 1906:** Railwaymen everywhere were well-known for their affinity to the famous British "pint". Gorton and neighbouring Openshaw were more than adequately served by Public Houses, or "Beer Houses" as some smaller establishments were known. There were, reportedly, along Ashton Old Road between Fairfield Street and Fairfield Wells, 39 pubs on one side of the road and 41 on the other! Doubtless generations of railwaymen had over the years frequented most of these establishments. Here is a fine view of one such: The Railway Hotel, a hostelry that stands (it is still there today) at the corner of Cornwall Street and Railway Street. Interestingly, the pub is situated astride the township boundary between Gorton and Openshaw. At the time this picture was taken the Landlord was James Inman who was...."*Licensed to sell by Law intoxicating liquors consumed ON or OFF the Premises."* John Jameson's Pure Pot Still Whiskey (sic) and Royal Huntsman Special Scotch Whisky are advertised on the lower windows – perhaps the populace were fond of a drop of "the hard stuff!" "Special Stout" is set in the frosted glass of the entrance doors, while over the doors appears "Dewars Perth Whisky." Spot the tiny inset pillar box and the notice advertising A GRAND CRICKET MATCH; this was held on Saturday, July 7th between Gorton and Newton Moor. Back to the railway: the bridge to the left leads over the GCR main line, while the Pallislade fence borders the entrance to the old Gorton station. Interestingly, the new station – further down the line and on the opposite side of the canal aqueduct – would open on the 25th of August 1906. The buildings in the background were part of the GCR's depot serving the Stockport branch of the Ashton canal. Notice the signals, not Mr.Bound's pneumatic variety, but of MS&L design – Starter for Gorton station box and Distant for Priory Junction.

*Manchester City Engineers' Archive*

**Priory Junction, mid-1930s:** A scene that typifies the former GC's suburban services out of Manchester London Road on the west side of Woodhead in pre-War days. F1 2-4-2 tank No.5586 heads a local train, bound for Glossop or Hadfield, past Priory Junction. We often hear the phrase "the glory of steam", but just look at the murk and smog in the background surrounding Gorton Loco. The train is made up of eight six-wheeled coaches plus a four-wheeler at the rear. A journey over the thirteen miles to Glossop might just be comfortable, but these sets were also used to bolster excursion trains. Photographs exist showing such trains en route from Manchester to the East Coast seaside resorts! Some thirty years earlier the Midland Railway had introduced close-coupled sets of bogie stock for its Manchester South District and Birmingham suburban services. Food for thought? *William Lees*

**Gorton shed, 1920s:** J10 0-6-0 No.5125 awaits the moment to have its tender filled with coal from the north side of Gorton's two-road coaler. Until the advent of mechanised coaling plants from around the late 1920s-early 1930s this was how coaling of locos was executed: wagonloads of coal were pushed up an inclined ramp into the coaling stage (one such can be seen behind the J10's cab), the wagon's side doors were opened and coal was shovelled by hand into small steel tubs or "skips". These were pushed forward along projecting rails (see photo) and the contents tipped into the empty tenders or bunkers. All-in-all a thoroughly heavy, dirty, dusty and unpleasant task for the poor souls whose job it was. Mercifully, Gorton was released from such tedium with the arrival of the "Cenotaph" (qv). Alas for neighbouring Heaton Mersey, and indeed pretty well all the depots over the former GWR system, such antediluvian practices lasted till the bitter end.

*W.H.Whitworth*

Frank Rushton served for 49 years with the GC, the LNER and BR, beginning work as a telephone lad at Gorton Loco just before the Grouping, in 1922. His father before him, Frank Rushton Senior, was also a Gorton footplateman and started at Gorton in the very first years of the Great Central, in 1899. The family's Gorton links were further strengthened by a son-in-law who worked for Beyer, Peacock & Co. until the demise of that great company in 1966. Frank Rushton Junior's recollections were compiled in 1980. The following year, 1981, Allan Brown, a member of the Manchester Locomotive Society, submitted the memoirs for publication in "The Mancunian", the society's journal. Frank Rushton's article provides a valuable insight into locomotive and train working; beginning in an age when Great Central engines and men still reigned supreme.

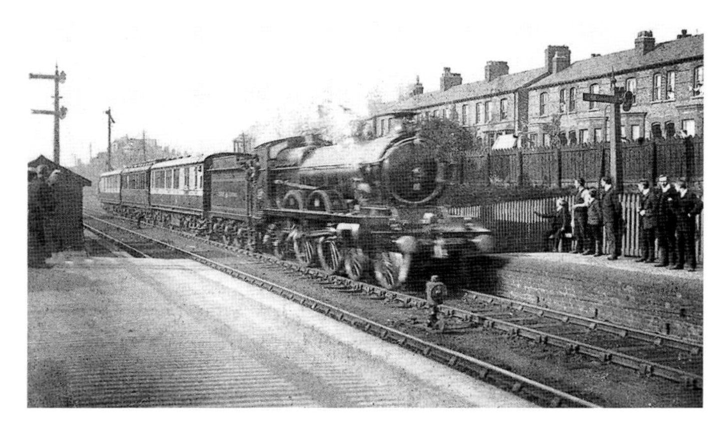

**Hale station, July 7th 1908: Frank Rushton's "King Edward". No.259 *King Edward VII* heads the Royal Train carrying the Prince & Princess of Wales en route from Chester to Stockport Tiviot Dale for the opening of Stockport Town Hall.** ***Author's collection***

In 1922 the Running Superintendent at Gorton was W.C.P.McClure. F.Hulme was Chief Clerk, P.Unsworth and J.L.Stopford were Locomotive Inspectors and E.Maugham was Shed Foreman. Prior to 1922 certain highlights stood out such as the run from Manchester over the GWR system to Plymouth with an Atlantic engine, the charge of Driver Stopford and Fireman J.Howard. Then there was the opening of Immingham Dock when Atlantic No.364 *Lady Henderson* worked the Royal Train and the large-wheeled 4-6-0 *Immingham* took the officials' train from Gorton Top Yard to Immingham for the opening driven by Jack Harrison. The opening of the new Town Hall at Stockport brought Atlantic No.259 *King Edward* (sic) on the Royal Train which was the charge of Driver Enoch Bell and Fireman Jack Howard with Loco Inspector J.L.Stopford. The 1913 "Directors" *The Earl of Kerry, Worsley Taylor, Walter Burgh Gair, Sir Berkeley Sheffield, Prince Henry, Prince George* etc. and Atlantics *Lady Henderson, Viscount Cross* (sic) and *King Edward* (sic) etc. worked the expresses to Marylebone and Cleethorpes. Then there were the 4-4-0 *Queen Mary* and *Queen Alexandra* Class, the "700" and "800" green passenger 4-4-0s, the small 0-6-0 "Black Goods" and the larger "Pom Poms", the 4-cylinder 4-6-0 "Lord Faringdons", the 2-cylinder "Glenalmonds", the "Sam Fay" 2-cylinder 4-6-0s and the "Fish Engines" of the "1109" Class. Drivers J.Langley and A.King were on the Oxford jobs with Atlantics.

Between 1922-1927 the "Valour" Class 4-6-0s had drivers E.Bell, T.Davies, J.J.Johnson, W.Davy, B.Goulden and Willoughby Lee on the London jobs and the "Directors" shared the work. Drivers W.Clark and Threadgold of Neasden with "Directors" 501 *Mons* and 504 *Jutland* worked alternate days on the 3.20 pm ex-London and 2.15 pm ex-London Road. Nos. 506 *Butler Henderson* and 507 *Gerard Powys Dewhurst* were also Neasden engines and the Atlantics had been transferred to Leicester, Woodford and Neasden. Gorton men worked the 5.25 am slow to Sheffield, the 8.20 am, 2.15 pm and 3.50 pm "Fasts" to London and the 3.53 pm Slow to Sheffield, then a fast Bradford-London to London and return trains between Sheffield and London. (One of these, the 4.55pm from Marylebone earned itself the nickname "Promptitude" on account of its excellent record for punctuality). The Newcastle-Bournemouth from Sheffield to Leicester was diagrammed into Gorton workings. Gorton also worked the 9.25 am, 11.22 am and 7.22 pm Central-Hull trains with "City" Class engines and the 1.35 am newspaper train with "City" Class or 4-cylinder Mixed Traffic 4-6-0 engines Various engines of the other pre-Grouping companies were also finding their way to Gorton. The "Boat Train" with Driver Jack Howard was worked by GER No.8535 from Manchester Central to Ipswich, alternating with Ipswich drivers J.Pack and J.Pinkney. Later the "Sandringhams" appeared, with Driver Howard getting 2809 *Quidenham*.

**B12s appeared in 1927 to work the "Boat Train" through to Ipswich. Jack Howard got No.8535. Here is the third B12 arrival. Seen on Gorton shed in 1928 is No.8538.** ***G.H.Platt***

The Sheffield, or No.2 Fast Train link had Drivers F.Cross, J.Fielding, R.Barlow, F.Bramwell, E.Fretwell and D.Bailey with their "City" Class engines whilst the London Goods Train link, nicknamed the "Pipe Train Link" because the trains were vacuum-fitted throughout, used 4-cylinder Mixed Traffic engines Nos.32, 33, 34, 470, 471 etc. with Drivers J.Rickards, J.Mason, D.Horne, J.Jones, T.Evans etc. The Hull goods was worked by 2-cylinder 4-6-0s Nos.52 and 53, Drivers Winstanley and Ashton working the 11.30 pm throughout from Ardwick to Hull. Grimsby and Lincoln fish and vegetable traffic was worked by 4-cylinder Mixed Traffic 4-6-0s and "Fish" engines of "1109" Class. Drivers J.Stopford, W.Pennington, T.Seaborne, J.Clark, W.McQuinn, J.Griffiths, J.Riley, C.Neave and A.Roberts were on these. The Mexborough coal train link and the Langwith and Annesley jobs were worked by Kitson 0-8-0s and Robinson 2-8-0s, the latter being in the majority. These trains were worked by Drivers H.Spencer, G.Bourne, J.Worthington, J.Leigh, E.Taylor, G.Massey, F.Credland and W.Hardman. The Barnsley Junction turn-back link had the same class of engine – with locomen S.Wright, R.Swallow, F.Abbott, J.Courtney, J.W.Newton and J.Parkinson. J.Howard (qv) and C.D.Philpott worked on Trial Trips; these involved preparing, trimming and testing engines fresh from Gorton Works, running them in and booking their defects. This sometimes involved two large sheets of repairs.

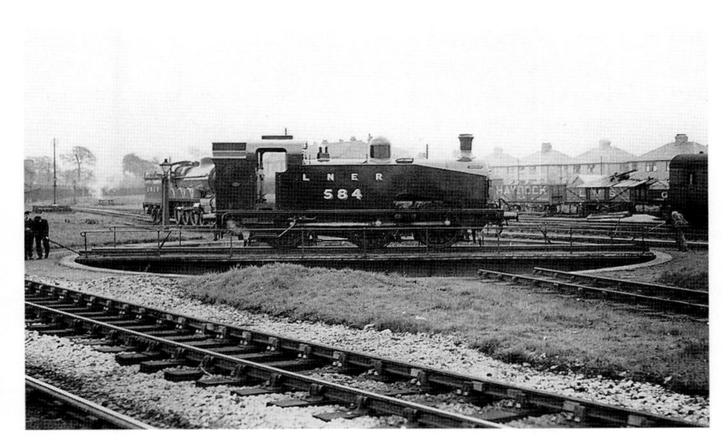


**April 1939: Trial Trips. Skelton Junction (on the Glazebrook to Godley line) was a convenient calling point with its large yard and turntable. J50/4 0-6-0 No.584, newly-built at Gorton, is seen in front of No.5196 (one of the two 6ft.9in.4-6-0s of 1903 & 1904) and fresh from a general repair at Gorton.** ***G.H.Platt***

Another notable link was the "Cover" or "Shining Light" link. This covered all the London jobs, both Fasts and Goods; the Lincoln and Grimsby jobs and Specials. These men signed the road for Scarborough and also worked Specials to Bridlington, Skegness and Mablethorpe. In the post 1927/28 period locomen allocated to this link were: W.Flanders, A.P.Warren, A.Booth, A.Goodwin, J.E.Hopley, G.Bagnall, W.Yeomans, A.E.Dakin and Ernie Calvert.

Push and Pull engines of the 2-4-2T type worked the Oldham, Stalybridge and Glossop lines and the Petrol railcar. Driven by Driver Jackson of Macclesfield, these trips were worked between Macclesfield and Bollington and in the rush hours went as far as Rose Hill. The Petrol railcar had been transferred from Aylesbury. Pilot turns were worked by "Black Goods" 0-6-2 Tanks on Ardwick, Guide Bridge and Dewsnap yards. A "Crab" tank engine (2-6-4) on the L&Y Ashton Moss Pilot also banked trains up to Ashton Moss from Guide Bridge.

The 5.25 pm and 6.10 pm meat trains ex-Huskisson to York were worked by 4-cylinder Mixed Traffic 4-6-0s. Gorton men took the engines light to Huskisson to work these jobs, engines Nos.71 and 72 with Drivers J.Birtwhistle and H.Wynne. If above a certain load, these trains were assisted from Godley to Wath Junction, generally by 0-6-0 "Pom Poms".

The 5.35 pm (Sundays) from Manchester central to Marylebone was first stop Sheffield and one day engine No.437 *Prince George*, when running through Penistone, collided with an L&Y tank engine. Driver Yeomans and Fireman Juby were on the footplate and Mr.McClure was on the train after his weekend visit home. He put the L&Y men and his own men in the Inspector's Office at Penistone and sent for a bottle of whisky to steady the men who had been shocked by the collision. Another of Mr.McClure's acts involved W.Howell who had been injured at Woodhouse when working an immigrant train and was put on the Gorton & Openshaw Pilot. Mr.McClure gave him a tank engine so he could rest his leg on the bunker end. T.Roebuck with a "Pom Pom" worked the Dove Holes job.

Engines 966 and 420, using pulverised fuel, worked by W.Baldwin and J.E.Mather, were on CLC work and the Ardsley jobs were worked by D.Mason and J.Sucker; the return job was with Driver Gilks of Ardsley.

Most of the jobs in the links were double-home jobs: working to London, Annesley, Langwith, Mexborough, Lincoln, Grimsby and York.

Also to Ipswich, Whitemoor and Bidston. A new Pullman train from Kings Cross to Manchester Central via Retford ran for a short time on 1925 and was worked by GN Atlantics. Driver Sparshott and another, whose name I have forgotten, lodged at Gorton. Local passenger work was done mostly by Joy valve 2-4-2 tanks, later replaced by the larger C13s. The drivers involved were G.Woodall, J.Knowles, J.Peyser, G.Clarke, F.Casey and J.Aveson. From Macclesfield shed worked Drivers C.Dale and W.Smithwith No.5593; whilst H.Shaun, J.Sleight and F.Ratcliffe of Hayfield had No.5735. W.Isaacs, W.Parker, J.Parker, H.Lewis, A.Cooper and A.Mansfield were at Dinting shed. Back at Gorton and G.Turner with a "Pom Pom" was on ballast trains, while G.Willerton worked the Gorton Top Yard Pilot with a GC "Hump" engine; later with a small GE side tank. J.Chamberlain was now on Trial Trips in place of J.Howard who had gone on to the "Boat Train" working and Driver Ernie Calvert was preparing ROD engines brought from the Government at Chester, Queensferry and Lancaster. F.Thomas (known as "Dodger") was on Trafford Park jobs wearing his bowler hat and a flower in his buttonhole.

**Driver J.Rickards' favourite: "Director" No.5510 *Princess Mary* takes the Fallowfield line at Chorlton Junction with an Up express c.early 1930s.** ***Author's Collection***

Around Gorton the noise of whistling was constant. Every movement had its whistle code to the Gorton Yard signalbox – a code off every road or position and routing to destination. I lived 20 minutes walk from the shed and at night could decipher movements made from these whistles.

The slump of the 1930s meant that men were transferred all over the LNER system and the younger-end cleaners and passed cleaners were out of work. I personally lost faith in the railways, having been reduced to a shed labourer in the sponge cloth workshops on Cornwall Street working in very bad conditions among caustic soda, steam and dirt. All sponge cloths from the Southern area of the LNER came to these shops for cleaning; they were boiled in tanks, washed in "Bradford" washers and dried again by means of hot air blown into a dryer which was heated by burnt refuse collected from the sponge cloths in the course of washing. The residual oil from these cloths was syphoned off, barrelled and used for point oil by the platelayers.

Prospects brightened in 1934 with firemen, passed firemen and passed cleaners returning to their own depots to be reinstated. Many older drivers had retired and there was a great movement of men in the links which was coupled with more work. Gorton got some A1s for a period such as *Victor Wild* and *Tracery,* whilst engines such as *Sir Frederick Banbury* were still coming to Gorton up the 1950s. I handled some of these as a passed fireman on the 3.50 pm Manchester London Road to Marylebone as far as Sheffield, Lodging jobs having been dispensed with during the war years. The "Sandringhams" and "Footballers" were also in evidence in the 1930s until 1947 with engines such as *Falloden, Manchester United, Huddersfield Town, Middlesbrough* and *Somerleyton Hall*, all Gorton engines. Driver A.Roberts had *Falloden* and D.Horner had *Somerleyton Hall*.

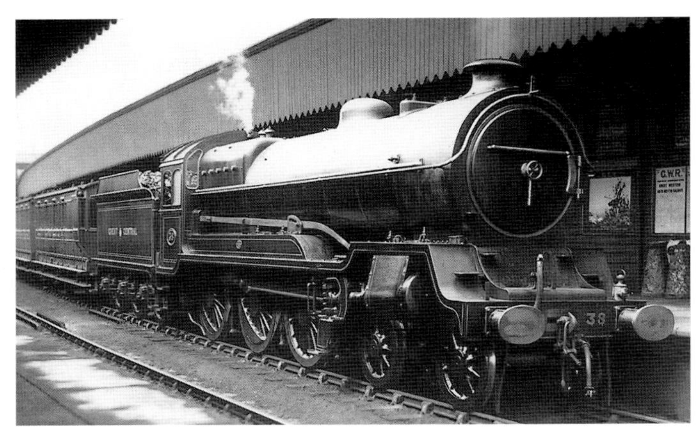

**Frank referred frequently to the Mixed Traffic 4-cylinder locos. Here is one such: No.38 seen at Guide Bridge on a local train. Note the 6-wheeled stock and the rather strange engine headcode.** ***P.F.Cooke***

K3s now worked most of the fast goods trains and NER Class Q7s and 3-cylinder mixed-traffic 4-6-0s were mixing with GC 2-8-0s and 4-cy;inder mixed-traffic 4-6-0s. The days before the 1939 war saw the Harwich Boat train linked with the Marylebone jobs and the "Sandringhams" and "Footballers" were on the work. But Driver J.Rickards remained with his GC "Director" No.5510 Princess Mary and later with No.5502 *Zeebrugge* having opted to retain this type. I often wonder if J.Rickards was the driver of No.5510 when it put up the record performance between London and Leicester. *(The run concerned was possibly the 3.20 pm Marylebone-Sheffield which averaged 56.8 mph between Marylebone and Leicester on an unrecorded date in 1932).*

Jim (Senior) Rickards did not take to the rough-riding "Footballers". He knew the London Road link like the back of his hand, having worked the London goods for many years before he went into the express passenger link. Driver G.Bourne was also in this link and could perform wonders with a "Director" or "Footballer", whilst Driver G.Glover was another example of a perfect fast train man – and there were many of the same calibre.

The "Valour" Class had been transferred to Immingham and Immingham men had one on their Cleethorpes-King's Cross turn.

Gorton Loco had been a very different place since the wet ash pit and coal hopper had been built and the shed was much cleaner. Ernest Maugham, the Shed Foreman, still reigned supreme and his exploits with the accident vans were well known throughout the district. I saw him tackle the crash in Woodhead Tunnel when Driver C.Walker, working a goods train, hit another inside the tunnel. The O4 ploughed its way underneath the guard's brake van and rammed several wagons into the roof. The conditions were terrible when clearing up this mess which happened about 4.00 am. Mr.Maugham collapsed about 6.00 pm after crawling about giving orders and instructions to his men. Following this, Mr.C.B.Kirk, the Running Superintendent at Gorton, took charge. The job was completed about 4.00 the next morning.

Another accident involving the newspaper train which was hauled by either the converted "Valour" 4-6-0 No.6167, or possibly one of the first B1s whose reverser was on the opposite side to any other engine. The engine ran backwards from the tunnel and was diverted into the loop, hitting a train standing there. Most of the trains were derailed and toppled over the banking into the river.

The old coal stage (at Gorton) having gone, along with the signals in the yard, one of the turntable pits round the back of the old stage was filled in. The pulverised fuel plant taken down from No.21 road making the place look more open. Another memory concerns the "Belgium" coach which I think was used for Belgian royalty at some time. This was used as an office for the running foremen: G.Carter, H.Howsley and Ted Footill along with the Loco Inspector J.L.Stopford. The coach was very ornate inside and it disappeared sometime in the early 1930s. The old signalbox in the yard was now being used as the Running Foreman's office, with its huge board recording the placings of engines all over the yard, the 20 shed roads, the paint shop, 21 and the old sand road. Records of engines when they arrived had to be "X day" washouts, trial trips from the works etc. Underneath this signalbox, with its levers taken out, was a mess room for locomen. These men would argue and debate all things from passing for driving to Union affairs. They were nicknamed "Lighthouse Lawyers", this old signalbox being named "The Lighthouse". Many men passed through this cabin and a few who stood out as "Lawyers" were, A.Berry, H.Clarke, F.Grey, E.Hall, J.Hardman, A.W.Milnes, H.Morton, C.Parker, J.Watson, F.Worsley and many more. There was a comradeship amongst these men and those before them that I don't think will ever exist again.

**The former shed yard signalbox, aka "The Lighthouse". The board on the box front reads: "Running Foreman's Office No.1". The mess room beneath was where Frank's "Lighthouse Lawyers" met to....."argue and debate all things".** ***William Lees***

Alderman Tommy Walker and T.H.Adams were members of Manchester City Council and had regular night turns to enable them to attend their various council duties during the day. Later, T.H.Adams, when he was a Loco Inspector, served as Lord Mayor of Manchester about the 1947 period. *(Records show that Thomas Henry Adams was Lord Mayor of Manchester from 1946-47 - Author).* Other men who served their council were J.Aveson, C.Parker, R.Boak, H.Turner and E.S.Jones.

The war years put an end to the "Lodging" jobs and Gorton lost its distinction of being the "mileage" depot of the Great Central. But long hours prevailed with work of various kinds.Evacuation specials from Liverpool to were handled by Groton men with K3 2-6-0s over the LMSR and Gorton men with 4-cylinder 4-6-0s and K3s worked from Edge Hill to Sheffield with trainloads of Yanks, Canadians, German and Italian POWs as well as Ambulance trains in each direction. I recall when firing for C.S.Pearce had to be run at not more than more than 25 mph all the way

to Edge Hill because it was loaded with seriously wounded Yanks.
Other wartime memories include the "black out" sheets around us on the footplate and the tank engines with sheets over their spectacle look-out glasses. Also the bad coal, dirty fires and the difficulty, sometimes, to keep going. Once a Kitson 0-8-0 had difficulty in the tunnel – I think the driver was E.Bottoms – and he had to drop the fire inside the tunnel. There was an express behind this failed train with King Haakon of Norway on board and it was delayed at Woodhead for over an hour!

**Woodhead, June 24th 1950: Like Frank Rushton, all drivers over Woodhead had their own special tale about the notorious tunnel. Doubtless the men on this O4 had theirs as well as their engine emerges into the daylight by the station.**
***Neville Fields/Manchester Loco Society***

"Green Arrow" (V2) engines were put on the Marylebones, hauling larger trains because of the reduced service. Gorton men changed footplates at Nottingham and what difficult times were had when boarding a "Green Arrow" with bad coal and dirty and clinkered fire on the return journey. With a heavy train, the long haul from Nottingham up to Annesley and through to Heath had the fireman struggling and sweating with the clinkered fire; sometimes a foot deep of solid clinker in parts of the box. The object was to get an air space on the grate, then take water on the troughs at Killamarsh. After this the run to Sheffield was spent building the fire up ready for the climb to Dunford Bridge – was the fireman glad to see Woodhead Tunnel!

Trial trip drivers in the period 1920s-1950s were J.Howard, Ernie Calvert, and Charlie Philpott. Charlie was known to the fitters in the works as "Split Pin Charlie" because of his keenness.

On March 8th 1945 the Royal Train ran from the LMS' side of Manchester London Road hauled by Class A4 No.4466 *Sir Ralph Wedgewood.* Driver A.Long and Fireman F.O.Rushton (Frank himself) with the H.O.Loco Inspector were on the A4 which was carrying King George VI and Queen Elizabeth (later the Queen Mother). The train left at 5.30 pm and ran non-stop via Woodhead to Sheffield where the loco took water. I do not know its destination, but I believe it was Scotland. It was a very heavy train, full of different personnel and great precautions were taken, including troops at every bridge along the route and the Home Guard who, throughout the war, had been stationed at Woodhead and had provided a full turn-out – all standing to attention. This brings back memories of the Home Guard during the blizzard of 1941 when men and trains were marooned on the bank and could not get forward or go back. Some train men arrived back home after being out for two days. During this time they were fed with porridge, bacon and tea by the Home Guard. **(Author's note: Frank recalled the Royal Train engine as being A4 No.4462 *William Whitelaw*. However, this is disputed by an observer who was at the station. It was rumoured at the time that a second A4, No.2509 *Silver Link* was on stand-by duty at Gorton. The reason for the use of the LMS' side of London Road was so that the royal party could board the train directly from their car on the centre carriage road adjacent platform 4 - this for obvious security reasons. No.4462 is recalled as appearing "in shining black").**

At the end of the war the "Green Arrows" were still on the London jobs, while "Footballers" worked the Liverpool, Hull and Cleethorpes trains. Gorton men were now changing footplates at Leicester with Neasden men after working the 8.20 am from London Road and the 9.00 am "Slow" from London Road to Sheffield. The loco from this train took the 10.00 am Bradford-Marylebone as far as Leicester. Low Moor men worked this train from Bradford to Sheffield and back again. I found that by going to Leicester and changing there with Neasden men a much better-conditioned engine was received. Men from each depot were handing over as if they were doing the entire journey themselves.

**Manchester Central, May 1949: Arthur Davies with Bill Flanders' "pet" - B1 No.61162 by the turntable at Manchester Central. Arthur's fireman was the young Bert Lloyd. The duo were waiting to work the 4.30 pm (ex-Liverpool Central) express to Hull forward to Sheffield Victoria at 5.27.** ***R.E.Gee***

B1 4-6-0s took the place of the "Green Arrows" and as loads were better there was a slight speeding-up. *We had the first "1100s", painted green, which were running through. Then we got a batch of "1080s" from North British works. Gorton was then allocated some of the splendid Vulcan-built engines: Nos.1155-1162, all painted green and these were allocated to Gorton men as follows: No.1155 – Dick Ball; No.1156 – Arthur Davies; No.1157 – A.G.Warren; No.1158 - Harry Sheppard; No.1159 – J.H.Smith; No.1160 – Arthur Orsler; No.1161 – W.Flanders; No.1162 – Arthur Jameson. ***Ernie Naylor records the first B1 to arrive was No.8301 *Springbok* in March 1943.**

At this time we were still going to Leicester, but instead of changing footplates, we came off and turned, retaining our own engines. When looked after, they performed some good work and were grand machines. Driver A.G.Warren and myself had No.1157 for 2 years and whilst No.1158 was the strongest, they were all good runners. When Arthur Davies retired, Driver L.Schofield took his place on No.1156 and when A.G.Warren went, Driver W.H.Bromley took over No.1157 with W.Williamson taking over from J.H.Smith on No.1159.

A trip to remember took place on a Sunday during heavy snow in the winter of 1947. The snow plough ran up the loop from Valehouse to Woodhead, the other roads being blocked. Driver Flanders on No.1161 at the head of the Up London followed on a time basis as no signals were being operated. Driver Warren and myself with No.1157 followed the

London with about a 10-minute margin on the Liverpool-Hull which we had taken over at Manchester Central. It was a reduced train of only 6 coaches. We had a full head of steam and engine on full traverse (cut-off) between Torside and Crowden. The snow was blowing over the rails and this reduced our speed to under 20 mph and sometimes to 15 mph, especially approaching Crowden. I thought we would never make it to Woodhead. This battle between the weather and machines was exciting and interesting and gave us a feeling of a job well done.

Time passed and one saw signs of electrification. Electric locomotives were being built in the erecting shop and the motors were installed in them at Dukinfield by Metro-Vick men. Driver training was taking place and Mexborough men started working trains to Dunford "Down" yard where they handed over to Gorton men with their O4s for the journey through the tunnel. Gorton men then started with Bo+Bo electrics attached to the front of the O4s hauling the O4 and the train to Crowden, thus giving the crew on the 2-8-0 time to get warmed up for the tunnel. The new tunnel was completed and the arrangements for switching from steam to electric went without a hitch. Drivers R.Hulley, T.Farrell, E.E.Newton, T.Clarke, P.L.Fletcher and J.Hollis were transferred to Reddish and worked all the fast trains between London Road and Sheffield (Guide Bridge for the (Manchester) Central jobs with Co-Co electrics. W.Harrison, F.Hilton, H.Beddoes, F.Latchford, H.Morton, H.Kennerley and others were stationed at Guide Bridge for working freights; the freight link having 48 drivers in all. The Glossop EMU trains were maintained by Drivers T.Haman, W.Tophill, W.Norbury, T.Creamer, R.W.Betts, W.Kay and W.Collins. After the electrification Gorton steam shed was much quieter. C13s worked the local passenger trains and A5 tanks worked the fasts between Central and guide Bridge. The CLC work remained plus the summer specials to Blackpool, Southport (Chapel Street) and Rhyl which were worked with a few B1s. Diesel multiple units then came for the branch passenger trains, the ex-GC engines went and in their place came a few Midland "Crabs" and "Derby 4s" which were all in a run-down state. Steam was dying: Gorton shed closed, but the Guide Bridge depot took its place. The yards around Guide Bridge were emerging as the hub for freight traffic on the east side of Manchester.

**Frank concluded:** "I have done my best to recall things that have appened during 49 years, but cannot put down everything – my memory is not as good as it was". Frank Rushton died in 1981.

**The author wishes to thank the Committee of the Manchester Locomotive Society, the Editor of "The Mancunian" and Allan Brown for their permission to re-publish Frank Rushton's article.**

**Gorton shed yard, c.1936:** The "Cenotaph" or mechanical coaling plant together with the wet ash pits had done much to ease the lot of shed labourers and loco crews. At Gorton, as at engine sheds everywhere, much of the engine preparation and disposal work was heavy, laborious and thoroughly unpleasant. This mid-1930s view of Gorton's coaler shows clearly the electric hoist and lifting platform for the loaded coal wagons whose contents were then tipped down into the bunker and from there into the ever-hungry loco tenders and bunkers. *William Lees*

**The B17s, both "Sandringhams" and "Footballers" had been a major part of footplate life at Gorton from late 1927 until the early war years. Here is No.61660 *Hull City* seen awaiting a works visit in mid-December 1949.** ***Author's collection***

**A typical Gorton pay check**

**Gorton Works, c.December 1906:** A Robinson Compound Atlantic Class 8E (thought to be No.365) is seen in the erecting shop. Suspended on chains and in the final stages of completion, the loco is still bereft of crossheads, connecting, coupling rods and front bogie. The livery appears to be "works grey" prior to final painting, though some engines appeared in this colour fully lined out for photographic purposes. Notice the usual workshop "Clutter" and the ready-formed footplate valances in the foreground. The overhead electric cranes were a product of Craven Brothers of Manchester and had a lifting capacity of 50 tons. No.365 was named Sir William Pollitt before October 1907; it was withdrawn as LNER Class C5 No.2898 in August 1947.

*Clarke & Hyde*

**Gorton Works, April 29th 1938:** Built for Fish traffic from the GC's ports of Hull and /Grimsby, this is No.5184 seen outside the works painted in gleaming unlined black during a general overhaul. Beyer, Peacock built eight of these 6ft.1in.engines in 1904; another six appeared two years earlier, a product of Neilson & Co. In June 1923 No.5184 had been rebuilt with a standard O4-type boiler of a bigger diameter to that as built. A later-pattern GC-style cab was fitted, but this was subsequently removed and the whole class was fitted with a Q4-type boiler. The rebuilding involved raising the bolier centreline by some nine inches, altering completely the engines' appearance. *Author's collection*

**Gorton Works, late GC days:** A look inside the erecting shops and into "3-Bay", part of the heart of the Gorton empire. Always entering boiler-first, locos here would be stripped for repair all the various classes of steam locomotive that served the Great Central. In the foreground is No.392 – a Robinson 8K (04) built in 1914. Ahead is a 4-6-0, the presence of a nameplate suggests Class 8F No.1097 *Immingham*; then follows an 0-6-0, an 11B 4-4-0 (D9) followed by a Parker Class 6A1 (J8) 0-6-0 of 1887/88 distinguished by its curved footplate. Further GC types abound, not all are clearly distinguishable, but a tank engine sits on the right-hand side behind a 4-6-0 or 4-4-2 tender engine. At the far end of the bay was a landing stage that led to the machine shop. Always present in this type of view are the great number of locomotive component parts with wheels and axles in particular in profusion here. Though seemingly strewn everywhere the parts were doubtless always returned to their rightful place. Notice the line shafting, the overhead power house that drove almost all of the shop machinery in this era. Antiquated by today's standards of course, but Gorton Works had been substantially re-equipped in the early years of the 20th century. *Author's collection*

**Gorton Works, Erecting Shop, October 1937:** Four separate jobs are under way in this view . Over to the left B7 4-6-0 No.5468 is undergoing a general repair. The loco is recorded as having received four new cylinders at its last visit here the previous year. Behind the B7 can be seen one of the CLC's Sentinel six-cylinder steam railcar No.602. This was one of four used by the Committee. The Sentinels were used on Liverpool-Stockport services and locally on services from Stockport Tiviot Dale to Altrincham on which they were known affectionately as "The Baguley Bus". From 1931 all four were based at Brunswick for services in the Liverpool area. No.602 continued working Liverpool to Gateacre and Warrington services until October 1944. All the Sentinels were withdrawn that year and No.602 was scrapped at Doncaster in October 1944. Lined up in front of the B7 and the railcar can be seen the coupled wheels from the B7 and in front those from a Gresley J39 0-6-0 which is seen taking centre stage. Undergoing a general repair, the loco is possibly No.2712 which is recorded as having undergone a general repair at Gorton from September 27th to October 23rd in 1937. *Author's collection*

**Gorton Works, paint shop, pre-WWI:** It was here in the paint shop that engineering excellence was turned into a splendidly-finished locomotive by men who could only be described as artists. Three Robinson engines present themselves in this scene – a picture oozing with perfection – and taken in an era that could only be that of the Edwardians and always looked upon as the heyday of the railways. On parade, left to right, are a "Sam Fay" 4-6-0 (or Class 1), a black-liveried 8F 4-6-0 or "Immingham" (number not known, but one from the sequence 1100-1104) and a Class 9K 4-4-2 tank engine. A slight blur on the mens' faces by the tank engine betrays the time exposure needed for the photography of almost a century ago. Notice the rudimentary lighting: gas piping suspended from a cross-fed supply with only the light of a naked flame to illuminate the shop.
*Great Central Railway/National Archives*

**Gorton shed yard, late 1924:** A most interesting picture taken on the cusp of the changeover from GCR to LNER. The view, dominated by the pulverised fuel plant and the manual coaling stage, shows well the mess and squalor brought about by the fire-dropping process. Before the arrival of the wet ash pits the spent contents of locomotive fireboxes were merely raked out and placed into heaps before being shovelled into wagons for disposal. Standing "on shed" that day were (l-r) No.548, an N5 0-6-2 tank; No.407 (behind), an O4 2-8-0 and off to the right none other than B3 4-6-0 No.1169 *Lord Faringdon.* Peeping out behind His Lordship and betraying the picture's LNER provenance, is No.438E, "Director" *Worsley Taylor.* *P.F.Cooke*

**Gorton shed yard, 1880s:** The limitations of contemporary photography have deprived us of any significant sight of the engines of Charles Reboul Sacré at work over the MS&L's principal routes. No.426 emerged from Gorton works in July 1877, one of 27 6ft.3in. 4-4-0s of Class 6B designed by Sacré, this being his first venture into the 4-4-0 genre, previous express engines being 2-4-0s. Ahrons records that the 4-4-0s "bore practically the whole burden of the Manchester, Sheffield and Lincolnshire main line work for many years..." A Gorton engine diagram book for February 1886 lists No.426 as being the charge of Driver W.Dean and Fireman A.Edlington (these may well be the men in our picture). The working shown is for the 6.45 am London Road to New Holland train.The men booked on at Gorton at 5.30 am; the train arrived at New Holland at 10.20, leaving again for Manchester at 11.15 and due back there at 3.00. The mens' duties for the day ended at 4.30 pm. The diagram lists 6¼ quarts of oil and ½ lb.of cottton waste being allowed. Ahrons confirms No.426 as being stationed at Gorton and mentions that the 6Bs did occasional work on the joint MS&L/GNR King's Cross expresses as far as Retford. The locomotives were built with Smith's non-automatic vacuum brake; notice the two ejector pipes on the smokebox side. The "Lighthouse" signalbox stands out clearly in the background. *Author's collection*

**Gorton shed, later 1930s:** B17 No.2845 *The Suffolk Regiment* was one of a quintet completed at Darlington Works in the summer of 1935, the final batch to appear with the short wheelbase GER-pattern tender. In this view taken along the back of the running sheds the 77-ton bulk of No.2845 is lifted at the rear by the Gorton sheerlegs over an inspection pit, the purpose of the exercise almost certainly being attention to the centre and rear axleboxes – rough riding and frame fractures proving to be the engines' Achilles Heel. The picture illustrates well the rugged nature of locomotive shed work and the fraught conditions under which fitting staff had to work. Imagine such a task in the depths of a wet Manchester winter's day! No.2845 was an Ipswich engine from new until October 1941 so her time on Gorton shed would be between through trips on the Harwich Boat trains between Manchester Central and her home town at the head of the celebrated "North Country Continental". *William Lees*

**Gorton Shed yard, mid-1930s:** We saw B17 No.2840 *Somerleyton Hall* earlier crossing Ashburys East Junction. But this second view of the same locomotive is irresistible. Cleaned, polished and ready to go, the engine poses for the camera with her driver proudly standing alongside. A somewhat copious quantity of coal is heaped up in the tender! Later on some of these GER-pattern tenders had impromptu coal guards added to aid stacking. This pile is well above the level of the cab roof and the reckoning is that *Somerleyton Hall* is off to work the "North Country Continental" from Manchester to Ipswich, the 216 mile journey taking just under six hours. An altogether remarkable feat of engine working. *William Lees*

**Gorton, Roundhouse, n.d:** This was the fabled roundhouse at Gorton viewed from the north side of the works looking to the main line. The houses along Railway Street can be glimpsed in the background. A plan dated 1851 shows the roundhouse as the main engine shed with a central turntable serving 17 roads. Latterly the building was used as a forge as part of the main forge and riveting shop. The building to the left was the works' electricity sub-station known as "the power house". Terry Holtby, a former Gorton apprentice who was at the works until closure, recalls a section of this building being used for chrome plating with "Henry" in charge. Terry remembers seeing the name plates for Bo+Bo *Archimedes* and Co-Co *Electra* being plated here. Henry had a sideline in selling cigarettes and toffees: "threepence ha'penny" being the going rate for one Lambert & Butler Domino cigarette. The building off to the right by the wagon was the office of the Blacksmith foreman – Mr.Addison.

*Author's collection*

Gorton, Roundhouse, November 21st 1965: Forming a stark contrast to the picture above, this view shows the roundhouse under demolition. Though the Beeching Report is largely associated with line and station closures, it had a wider remit than is sometimes realised. Beeching brought his former ICI colleague, Sir Steuart Mitchell, out of retirement to make a review of railway workshops. The result was a reduction in their number from 28 to 16, with Gorton as one of the casualties. Mitchell's review showed an annual "benefit" of £4M alongside a mere 3% overall benefit. *W.A.Brown*

**Gorton shed, mid-1930s:** A splendid panorama of the running shed in an age well before WWII when GCR locomotive classes held sway with none of the influx of LMR and other types that typified the shed's latter days up to closure. GC enthusiasts can amuse themselves by attempting identification of all the locomotives on parade. No less than twenty roads were spread out within the main confines of the shed here, notice the small sign in the foreground by the bowler-hatted figure reading "18 &19". The identity of the official-looking gentlemen is, sadly, unknown though he may well be the shed foreman as the photographer, William Lees appears to have had unfettered access to railway premises and was obviously a well-known visitor. *William Lees*

**Gorton & Openshaw, April 19th 1950**: N5 0-6-2 tank No.69260 pauses with a stopping train, probably bound en route via Guide Bridge to Glossop and Hadfield. The line from Ardwick to Hyde Junction through Gorton was widened to four tracks in 1905/06. This resulted in the re-siting of Gorton station from its original position further west towards Manchester. The bridge in the background is the aqueduct carrying the Stockport branch of the Ashton canal over the railway. The N5 tanks were a development from 1891 by Thomas Parker of his earlier 0-6-2 design (N4) of 1889. *Neville Fields/Manchester Loco Society*

**Beyer, Peacock & Co., Gorton Foundry, September 29th 1928:** No work centred on Gorton would be complete without at least some coverage of the products of world-famous locomotive builders, Beyer, Peacock & Co. The weekend of September 29th & 30th saw the Gorton Foundry hosting a locomotive exhibition in aid of Manchester medical charities. The centre of attraction appears to be LNER locomotive No.8580. This was the last example of the celebrated Great Eastern design of 4-6-0, arguably the most successful of the British inside-cylinder 4-6-0s. As GER Class S69 the locos became LNER B12 and the design was perpetuated with the company ordering ten engines which were built by Beyer, Peacock between August and October 1928. From 1927 the B12s had become regular visitors to Gorton when they began to work the celebrated "North Country Continental" from Manchester through to Ipswich, a distance of 216 miles. The LNER B12s differed from their GER predecessors in having an extended smokebox, Lentz poppet valves as opposed to the piston valves in the previous engines, as well as sundry differences. No.8580 was the last of the ten Beyer engines, happily the first of these, LNER No.8572 survives in active preservation today. Off to the left of the scene another Beyer product is displayed complete with viewing platform above the tender: this is the Ljungström turbine condenser locomotive. Also on show that weekend were two Garratts, one for the Nitrate Railways of Chile, the other for the Kenya and Uganda Railways. In the background can be seen the outlines of the erecting shops at neighbouring "Gorton Tank". Fashion-conscious readers will observe that hats were *de rigeur* in those days! Thanks to Beyers' efforts the sum of £278 was raised for the charities that weekend with no less than 11,000-12,000 visitors attending on the Sunday. *Collection of Joe Lloyd*

**Fairfield, c.mid-1930s:** B3/2 4-6-0 No.6168 *Lord Stuart of Wortley* sweeps through Fairfield station on the Up fast line with an express for Marylebone. In 1929 No.6168 had become one of four of the class to be rebuilt with Caprotti valve gear in an effort to improve coal consumption. Though the engine has been rebuilt and the coaching stock is comprised of Gresley vehicles, there is enough atmosphere to instill a pure Great Central flavour. Notice the splendid roadside buildings above the train and the two styles of platform awnings. Only a concrete hut betrays any tangible sense of modernity. *William Lees*

## FAIRFIELD FOR DROYLSDEN

Fairfield station sat once upon a time in what was known as the Township of Audenshaw, close to the border with Manchester. Today it resides in what is now Tameside, a sprawling metropolitan borough that encompasses neighbouring Ashton-under-Lyne, Droylsden and Stalybridge. The suffix "for Droylsden" was, in typical railway fashion, a trifle disingenuous, the district in question being some way off, on the north side of Ashton New Road. Aside from the railway, Fairfield is best known for its famous Moravian Settlement established in the township as far back as 1783; the Moravians being the oldest Free Church in Northern Europe. Fairfield became a focal point on the MS&L main line when the 6½ mile connecting line opened in 1892 from here down through Fallowfield to Chorlton-cum-Hardy in South Manchester. There it joined the Midland's main line to Derby out of Manchester Central. Fairfield station saw three distinct phases: the original station, dating from 1841, was sited around a quarter of a mile east of a second station; this had opened in 1892 (when the "Droylsden" suffix was added) commensurate with the opening of the Fallowfield line. When the railway between Ardwick and Hyde Junction was widened in the early years of the last century this second station was rebuilt to accommodate no less than six platforms. After local traffic through Fallowfield ceased in 1958 two platforms fell into disuse. Further rationalisation came in 1973 when the four-track alignment from Gorton through to Guide Bridge was done away with. Only two platforms remain today bringing the wheel of progress back, full circle, to 1841! Fairfield's most famous resident, at least as far as the railway goes, was the GCR's locomotive engineer, J.G.Robinson. "JGR" arrived at nearby "Boothdale Villa" from Heaton Chapel, near Stockport, in 1903. Here the Robinson family resided until 1915 when they upped sticks and moved to nearby "Mere Bank House", their home until the end of the Great Central in 1922.

**Fairfield station, July 13th 1974:** The building exterior as it was before the days of glass and plastic "bus shelters." This was the exterior of the later (1892) station built to accommodate the MS&L's new railway via Fallowfield to Chorlton-cum-Hardy. This was a *de-luxe* railway insofar as passenger accommodation went. The architecture had much in common with the four Fallowfield line stations: inlaid brickwork, neat little roof gables with stone lintels below with the station's name and opening year inscribed underneath. And don't miss that lovely little cupola on the roof and the bridges – blue engineering brick with inset panels and dressed stone copings. Viewed from the south side of Booth Road, the station buildings are, alas, in their death throes and soon the demolition men will be arriving.

*Harold.D.Bowtell/Manchester Loco Society*

**Approaching Fairfield, June 11th 1948:** In contrast to *Witherslack Hall*, seen earlier at London Road, here is another of the combatants in the 1948 loco interchange trials: Southern Railway "West Country" Pacific No.34006 *Bude*. The train is the 8.25 am London Road to Marylebone and it would appear that *Bude* acquitted herself admirably time-keeping wise. Never had Woodhead seen steam motive power like this!

*J.D.Darby/Manchester Loco Society*

**Fairfield for Droylsden, June 26th 1948:** No mistaking where we are! C13 No.7412 rolls into Fairfield with a four-coach local train, probably a Manchester London Road to Macclesfield Central service. The train is on the Up Fast line; the Slow lines are behind the island platform over to the right. Apart from the LNER nameboard, the station is still in pure GCR condition complete with gas lamps and the distinctive semaphore signals.

*Neville Fields/Manchester Loco Society*

**Fairfield Junction, mid-1930s:** "Director" Class D10 No.5438 *Worsley Taylor* comes along the Up Slow line with an excursion working. Comprised of eleven 6-wheeled coaches the ensemble appears to be an 8-coach Glossop and Hadfield set strengthened in front by a further three vehicles; the third of which looks ex-works with its pristine-painted sides and white roof. The train is likely to be bound for one of the East Coast seaside resorts: Cleethorpes, Mablethorpe, Skegness and Yarmouth being popular destinations. A great deal of such traffic was dispatched over Woodhead in those days, journey times varying between around 3-4 hours or more. Perhaps before we make too many complaints about modern rolling stock - hands up all those readers who would like a lengthy trip in coaches such as these *and* without a lavatory! Signalling and modelling buffs will no doubt admire the splendid array of signals here – recently converted from pneumatic to electro-pneumatic operation they read (l-r): Down Fast to Down Branch, Down Fast home, Down Slow to Down Branch, Down Slow to Down Fast, Down Slow home. *William Lees*

**Fairfield Junction, September 9th 1950:** 04/3 No.63679 barks over the junction as it comes off the Fallowfield line with a train of wagon empties, though take a look at the fourth wagon which appears to be still loaded. The train typifies traffic over Woodhead and, although this working will probably be bound for Dewsnap sidings or Mottram yard for sorting prior to onward movement; coal traffic it was that kept Woodhead alive and busy.

*Neville Fields/ Manchester Loco Society*

# THE FALLOWFIELD LINE

**Wilbraham Road, July 22nd 1938:** B7 4-6-0 No.5477 clears Wilbraham Road station with the Down Orient Line Special - working No.5255.Run in conjunction with the Orient Line's Norwegian cruises, the trains ran to and from Marylebone and Manchester Central to Immingham's Eastern Jetty passenger station. Through connections were provided also from Liverpool and Glasgow. The London train was comprised of about (sic) 10 coaches including Reastaurant cars; those from Manchester about 8 including Restaurant car and large van (sic). The train here will have left Immingham at 10.25 am and was due into Manchester Central at 1.48 pm.

*William Lees*

**Chorlton Junction c.1928:** No.5424 *City of Lincoln* (now Class B2) has come off the Fallowfield line with a Down express, probably from the East Coast. Clearing the St.Werburgh's Road overbridge (structure No.16) the train will now gather speed for the last 3½ miles or so of its journey into Manchester Central. The train is composed mostly of GC Clerestory stock, while the locomotive appears in the second version of the apple green livery lined black and white.A curiosity here was the distant arm below the Branch home; this was added during the WWI to aid the passage of coal empties along the Fallowfield line. After closure in 1988 the railway through here was re-instated to open in July 2011 as part of the Manchester Metrolink system. The same viewpoint today sees yellow trams passing by. *Sic transit gloria mundi!* *G.H.Platt*

## The author remembers

For most enthusiasts it is surely the early memories of childhood that are the strongest. At around age five or six, visits to Dorothy Smith, a friend of my mother's – such people were always "Aunties" in those days – found me spellbound in the back garden of No.15 Egerton Road South in Chorlton-cum-Hardy, a house that backed onto the Fallowfield line just east of Chorlton Junction. Here, this child, for we enthusiasts are all endowed with a Peter Pan gene, remembers clearly the sight of brown coaches hauled by a green engine flashing past the bottom of that magical garden.

Despite its strong connections with the Woodhead route, the Fallowfield line was not an early railway. Not until the 1880s did the MS&L spawn ideas of a connection from its main line from Manchester London Road to Sheffield across south-east Manchester to join the new Manchester South District Railway of the Midland into Manchester's Central station. Using the MS&L (Additional Powers Act dated September 25th 1886) a new railway – some 8 miles long was planned to link in with the CLC's Liverpool line at Old Trafford and close to the (then) new Manchester Central station.

In the event, the new line, 5 miles, 2 furlongs and 3 chains long, was built through what was then a largely open landscape. From Fairfield, a shade under 3¾ miles from London Road the line took a south-westerly course to join the South District line at Chorlton-cum-Hardy; though the junction was given the plain prefix of "Chorlton". Four stations were provided; from west to east these were: Alexandra Park (re-named "Wilbraham Road" from July 1923), Fallowfield, Levenshulme ( "Levenshulme South" from September 1952) and Hyde Road. The main contractor for the line was J.D.Nowell of Manchester who had quoted a price of £138,800. Construction was undertaken from both ends of the line, the first sod being cut in late January 1887. Nowell is known to have used four Manning Wardle 0-6-0s on the Fallowfield contract, these were: Amy, Beatrice, Gertrude and Trent. The railway was opened in two stages: from Chorlton Junction through to Fallowfield on October 1st 1891 and from there to Fairfield on May 2nd 1892. So was born what officialdom entitled The Manchester Central Station Railway or ever-after "The Fallowfield Line".

**Leaving Chorlton Junction, 1950s:** Clear signals from the Chorlton Junction and Wilbraham Road signalboxes give the driver of an unidentified 04/6 the "right away" along the rising 1-in-340 with an Up train of coal empties probably bound for Dewsnap sidings or Wath yard.. The "Peter Pan" garden belonged to one of the houses off to the right.
*N.F.W.Dyckhoff*

**Leaving Chorlton Junction, 1913**: In stark contrast to the picture above, this view reveals how much open land in South Manchester had been swallowed in the post-WWI period onwards by urban development. Robinson Atlantic Class 8J, the solitary 3-cylinder rebuild with Walschaerts valve gear, No.1090 runs through what was then farmland with the 3.20 pm express ex-Manchester Central to Cleethorpes and Harwich - possibly the earliest known photograph of that celebrated train "The North Country Continental". Dividing at Sheffield Victoria the Cleethorpes portion was due in at 6.55; the Harwich at 9.30. Notice the three 6-wheelers forming the front part of the train (probably for Cleethorpes); doubtless passengers would welcome a few breaths of sea air on arrival after an almost 5-hour incarceration!
*G.M.Shoults/Manchester Loco Society*

## Raison d'être

The purpose of the new line was threefold: to give the MS&L access rom its main line over Woodhead (the London Extension was still in its ormative stage then) to the newly-opened Manchester Central station nd, in consequence, to ease pressure over at London Road – where he MS&L were joint tenants with the LNWR and possessed only three latforms of their own. Thirdly, to tap the potential suburban rail traffic n Whalley Range, Fallowfield, South Levenshulme and the Hyde Road reas – the latter fringing on to the districts of Reddish and Denton. Jpon the opening of the Fallowfield Line, the section – 2 miles and 3 hains long – from Chorlton Junction to Throstle Nest Junction (where he Liverpool-Manchester line was joined) was transferred to CLC wnership, the latter being comprised of the MS&L, the Midland and he GNR.A later connection, a curve opened in 1906 from the CLC line t Throstle Nest South Junction into Manchester Central connected with he Liverpool line at Trafford Park Junction. The new connection thus nabling Manchester Central to be by-passed. The GNR had been given unning powers over MS&L lines north of Nottingham – which of course ncluded Sheffield to Manchester. This was a *quid pro quo* for the GNR ropping their opposition to the MS&L's London Extension in and around he Nottingham area.

**Below) Wilbraham Road station, June 28th 1957:** The main building vas sited on the corner of Alexandra Road South and Mauldeth Road. The paciousness and solidity of the brick-built structure shows up well in this iew. Notice the distinctive cast iron cupola on the roof and the "Alexandra Park" name set in stone above the entrance to the booking hall. What style, ut truly, a building that never fulfilled its potential. Hough End fields lie cross Mauldeth Road West in the background. *W.A.Brown*

## Details of the stations

High hopes indeed must have been entertained by the MS&L for local passenger traffic on their new railway. The main station buildings were quite handsome affairs with red brick facings; over the entrances curved stone arches were set, with the station's name and "1891" or "1892" inscribed as appropriate in an oblong stone block; stained glass windows above were topped by a high red-tiled impressive roof atop of which was set a cast iron cupola complete with flagpole; an altogether thoroughly handsome ensemble. What a contrast to the almost shed-like appearance of the LNWR's new standard wood-built station structures on their neighbouring Styal line opened some two decades later! Walking in, Victorian feet trod on parquet flooring which led across either side from the booking office down two-tier glazed wooden footbridges to platform level. Here, gas lamps with attractive tulip-shaped bases illuminated the platforms through glass bearing the name of each station. Passenger accommodation and buildings differed slightly at each station. Alexandra Park and Levenshulme were almost identical, being built by the same sub-contractor (by the name of Shaw) Fallowfield, though similar, had wholly brick-built buildings at platform-level compared to those at Alexandra Park and Levenshulme. Fallowfield station, costing a substantial £13,025, was built by J.D.Nowell. Curiously, Hyde Road was different from all three others: it was sited above road-level on an embankment and had brick-built accommodation on both up and down sides of the line, these fronted onto timber platforms; the other three having brick bases. Approaching Hyde Road the line crossed the Great Central & Midland Joint line from Romiley Junction to Ashburys East Junction via Belle Vue, a connection that had opened in 1875. At a junction just beyond Hyde Road the Fallowfield line split at Hyde Road Junction to form a triangular arrangement. Going east the line joined the MS&L's main line at Fairfield where a new station was completed upon the opening of the new line, the site having moved down 30 chains to accommodate the new railway. Curving west from Hyde Road Junction the MS&L line was joined at Gorton Junction, just slightly east of the station there.

**Wilbraham Road, September 6th 1947:** B1 No.1188 resplendent in lined apple green livery passes the goods yard with the 10.40 am Manchester Central to Hull express. Originating in Liverpool these expresses, along with the Boat train to Harwich, formed a staple pattern of long-distance workings from the line's very first days until diversion to Manchester Piccadilly in 1963. When this photograph was taken No.1188 was a new engine, having been completed at Vulcan Foundry just two months earlier. *R.E.Gee*

## Alignment and gradients

Leaving the Midland line at Chorlton Junction the railway was on a more or less constantly rising gradient. Beginning at a gentle 1-in-340/560/378 towards Fallowfield it was from there that the alignment steepened: at 1-in-100/1-in-80 towards Levenshulme, easing briefly before rising again at around 1-in-100 towards Hyde Road Junction. A contemporary observer of the local scene, the late Eric Rose, described how the sound of a GN Large Atlantic (C1) could be heard for miles around as the driver opened his machine up after clearing Chorlton Junction. At Fallowfield a banking engine was kept on standby to help give freight trains a push up the bank towards Levenshulme. In 1924 none other than Gresley Pacifics were recorded on banking duties here! A contemporary observer, Eric Dalton, noted No.2548 on October 2nd and No.2551 similarly engaged on December 11th and 22nd. Further Pacifics appearances were noted during the Second War, along with an ex-NER Class Z Atlantic being deployed as well. A water tank was provided at Fallowfield at the end of the up platform and to this day the bottom of the girders of the overbridge beyond Fallowfield station bear the ravaging marks of corrosion caused by the blasts of countless harsh steam exhausts over the years. In the autumn of 1961 on a showery evening I was observing the scene in the signalbox at Levenshulme South when a Brunswick (Liverpool) to Dewsnap freight was signalled from Chorlton Junction. After some time and still no sign of the train, the signalman, Ernie Thompson, and myself heard the very slow and unsteady roar of a steam engine's exhaust. Coming into view down by the station was a Black 5 travelling tender-first and almost slipping itself to a standstill on the bank. So slow was the train's progress that I had ample time to nip down to the trackside, select a suitable exposure – the light was fading – and take a photograph!

## A Royal show – July 1930

Rural life in England and Wales has been enriched and coloured by outdoor shows of one kind and another for generations. The Royal Agricultural Society of England (RASE) was established back in 1838 and has held annual shows, wars excepting, almost ever since. RAS shows were held on the fringes of most major cities; the first was at Oxford in 1839. Prior to 1930 the society had visited Manchester no less than three times: in 1869, 1897 and 1916. The two nineteenth century shows were held on land close to the River Irwell, fringing on to the CLC's Liverpool-Manchester line in Old Trafford. The 1916 show had been held on Hough End fields (qv) and it was to this location that the RAS was to return for their 89th show, held in July 1930. Access to the site was conveniently close to Wilbraham Road station and to expedite the rapid unloading of animals and machinery the LNER embarked on a complete rebuilding of the existing small goods yard. Very unusually, a direct (facing) connection off the Fallowfield line was made at the west end of Wilbraham Road station's down platform and a comprehensive rebuilding and enlargement of the yard was made. Siding provision was doubled – from two short dead end roads to four; two being built around island loading docks 650 ft.long and 50 ft. wide with a capacity for 33 vans on either side. The tracks paralleled the main line before re-connecting with it short of the Withington Road overbridge (structure No.29) some 400 yards distant from the station itself. This connection was worked by a ground frame, electrically released from the signalbox. Apart from the cost of the new trackwork, cart roads and loading docks, the station area had to be partially re-signalled. A replacement 28-lever frame (reportedly of ex-GN origin) had to be shoehorned into the signalbox, replacing the previous frame which had only 15 levers. Despite what must have been a considerable outlay, the LNER obviously thought the expense worthwhile. The show, held from July 8th-12th attracted 3138 assorted animals, 901 head of poultry and 443 farm implements and items of machinery. Three weeks before the show opened, 1100 wagons of implements and goods were dealt with at Wilbraham Road and during the weekend prior to opening 500 wagons conveying the livestock arrived there. Four express trains each way called especially for the show, although the Duke of Gloucester – the RAS' Patron who opened the show – arrived by air! No less than 300 railway vehicles were used to despatch the various items when the show closed.

15 trains were needed, leaving between 6.00 pm on Saturday and 4.00am on Sunday at a headway of 45 minutes. A busy night over Woodhead! RAS archives describe the event as a success with a particular vote of thanks going to the City of Manchester for their generous help and assistance. Alas, for the railways though, the 1930 show was the high watermark for rail involvement with these events; road traffic took over all movements for future annual shows.

**Wilbraham Road, 1930: (Top)** A busy scene showing the preparation for the new trackwork required for the facing point connection and subsequent new layout for the much-enlarged goods yard for the forthcoming RAS show. No less than 14 p-way men are caught at work in this picture. Doubtless taken for one of the Kemsley newspapers the caption reads: "*Even the railways lines are being relayed at Wilbraham Rd station Alexandra Park M/c in anticipation of traffic during the Royal Show week.*" Waistcoats and flat caps appear to be *de rigeur*; cravats seem optional! One can only wonder at the cost of such a project today and all for a mere one week's extra traffic. *William Lees*

**(Left)** The completed central loading dock looking east towards the station. Note the prepondrence of horse power, both horse-drawn and in horse boxes!
*R.D.Pollard/Manchester Loco Society*

**Wilbraham Road, Royal Show July 1930:** The LNER, ever-keen to garner publicity from an event, erected this "Inquiry Office" at the entrance to the yard and loading platform. Groundsmen appear to be putting the finishing touches to the surrounding turf, while a spectator gazes at the hoardings. Places all served by the company are advertised: Walton-on-the-Naze, Cromer, Harrogate, Norwich and York appear along with sailings from Harwich to the Belgian Coast (sic), though such a delight must have seemed an eternity away to farmers from the English rural districts in those days.
*R.D.Pollard/Manchester Loco Society*

**Wilbraham Road, Royal Show, July 1930:** The show received good coverage in the LNER's house magazine and was well illustrated. Precise dates for our pictures are not available, but the magazine reported that the process of delivering the various implements for display took three weeks prior to opening on July 8th and involved 1,100 wagon-loads. Livestock arrived at Wilbraham Road during the preceding weekend and involved nearly 500 wagons. Here is one such: a mobile crane has lifted two crates onto a horse-drawn wagon. From here it will be a short trot up the incline, a right turn into Alexandra Road and across Mauldeth Road West into Hough End Crescent and into the showground. All such operations had, of course, to be reversed when the show ended!
*R.D.Pollard/Manchester Loco Society*

## FROM THE MANCHESTER EVENING NEWS & CHRONICLE

July 7th: Stage set for £2M "Royal" – Manchester's bid for record.
July 8th: A crowd of 5,000 had gathered outside the showground waiting for the Duke in drizzle conditions. (Admission on the first day was 10/-).
July 9th: England recaptured a gold cup from America at the RAS in Manchester today when 3 young farmers (2 of them girls) won the International Dairy Cow judging competition.
July 10th: Depression's heavy blow to "Royal". Only 17,769 visitors have arrived (compared to 37,073 at Harrogate last year).

**Wilbraham Road, Royal Show, July 1930:** We complete our coverage of the Royal Show with this study of a fine beast at work. On the opposite side of the loading platform a horse-drawn provender wagon is seen unloading feed beside an ex-GER Hounds Van; in front is a 6-wheeled teak-bodied vehicle with prominent ducket, but of unknown origin. Though only a mere three miles or so from Manchester city centre, these delightful scenes have a wonderful rural flavour; sad that such events have long gone from suburbia nowadays.

*R.D.Pollard/Manchester Loco Society*

**Wilbraham Road, February 4th 1927:** We step back in time just over three years to look at a typical daily working over the Fallowfield line: this is the 11.22 am express from Manchester Central to Barnetby. The crisp winter air highlights the exhaust of ex-GN Atlantic Class C1 No.4412 as she storms through the station in readiness for the climb towards Hyde Road Junction. No.4412 was one of ten C1s that were transferred from former GN depots to Sheffield's Neepsend shed between 1923-25. Disliked at first by the GC men, the engines became firm favourites and put up some outstanding work. Though not technically perfect, this picture captures brilliantly well the memories of the late Eric Rose of these workings (qv). Worthy of a mention is the GC signal and splendid little MS&L-pattern signalbox. The signalman watching the train pass is Jack Smith who is mentioned elsewhere in our feature.

*G.H.Platt*

**Alexandra Park, c.pre-1912:** A mere handful of pictures of trains in the pre-Group era on the Fallowfield line have come down to us. Here is one such and a bonus inasmuch as it shows a local train complete with the infamous 6-wheeled coaches that remained a feature of these workings for so long. Drawn by Atlantic Class 8B (C5) No.361 the train is seen in the Up platform at what was then still Alexandra Park station. No.361 was one of eight Atlantics built by the GCR themselves at Gorton in 1906. It received a superheater boiler and piston valves in March 1912 and was withdrawn in February1949. In the background, on Athol Road, can be glimpsed some of the handsome late Victorian houses built in and around the Whalley Range area; this was middle-class Manchester to whose travelling sensibilities the MS&L hoped to appeal. *Collection of Norman Spilsbury*

**Wilbraham Road, February 18th 1938:** A local train of a totally different nature to that shown above is depicted here as B17 No.2865 *Leicester City* pauses with the 12.10 from Manchester Central to Guide Bridge. Notice that the train is made up of main line stock: this was one of two such workings that plied the Fallowfield line each day, diagrammed to obtain maximum use of engine and train. The loco will have arrived in Manchester Central at 11.16 as the 8.02 am express from Leicester Central - appropriately enough!. The coaches left Cornbrook carriage sidings at 11.33. On arrival at Guide Bridge, No.2865 will return light engine to Central, due in at 1.17 pm. It will then be diagrammed to work the 2.00 pm express to Liverpool, this train being the 7.25 am from Harwich Parkeston Quay. *William Lees*

**Wilbraham Road, February 4th 1927:** Not a remarkable scene, but a small part of a jigsaw that made up the traffic kaleidoscope that was "Woodhead". N5 0-6-2 tank No.5543 goes about its business doing the daily shunt or "Pilot". Working from Guide Bridge, the "Pilot" will have called at Fairfield, Levenshulme and Fallowfield before moving on from here via Chorlton-cum-Hardy to Deansgate yard, adjacent to Manchester Central. All pretty mundane, most of the work involved moving wagonloads of coal. Notice the sign above the hut on the right-hand side: "R.Taylor & Co, Coal & Coke Merchants" and the waiting horse and cart alongside. No.5543 was an 1894 product of Beyer, Peacock & Co. Seen here still carrying her Robinson chimney, the engine lasted until 1955. *G.H.Platt*

**Wilbraham Road, February 2nd 1938:** A powerful, low-angle shot showing Langwith Junction's O4 No.6636 approaching the station with a Down freight, reportedly a working bound for Deansgate Goods, though no details have been recorded. Services to and from the former GNR's Manchester goods depot centred chiefly on trains to and from King's Cross, Ardsley and Colwick (though the latter traversed the Midland's South District line from Chorlton Junction and over the Dore & Chinley ("Hope Valley") route to reach Chesterfield and on via Codnor Park). No.6636 was built by the North British Loco Co. in 1919. One of the ROD series of Robinson 2-8-0s, she was purchased for use by the LNER in August 1927 becoming a member of Class O4/3. No.6636 was rebuilt to Class O1 in 1946. *William Lees*

## Inaugural local passenger services

In 1891, when the first section of line opened, a service of 23 up and 24 down stopping trains was provided. Even on Sundays a service, five trains each way, was provided. This was before Manchester's electric trams came into service (June 1901) and the suburban railway in South Manchester became disadvantaged. Some of the locals provided a "circular" service from Manchester Central to London Road, others went as far as Guide Bridge, while two trains each day went as far as Stalybridge via Guide Bridge, Dukinfield and Ashton (Park Parade) with one through service to Oldham (Glodwick Road). The MS&L appears to have been a big user of 6-wheeled passenger stock for its local trains in and around Manchester. Such antediluvian stock lasted until well into the 1930s (qv) on both Guide Bridge and Glossop line services from both Central and London Road. Locomotive power was, for the most part, handled by the Parker Class 3 (LNE F1) 2-4-2 tank engines – used on the Fallowfield line from its opening. This was in distinct contrast to the 9-coach formations of Bain close-coupled bogie carriages hauled by the beefy-looking Deeley 0-6-4 tanks that appeared on the Midland's South District services from the early years of the twentieth century. For the record, on the line's opening an annual season ticket from Fallowfield to Manchester Central cost £6.00 (First Class) or £3.16/- (Third Class).

## Later local passenger workings

As was the case in many areas, the local passenger services were pruned in the First War never to regain their pre-1914 peak. Until the outbreak of the Second War, local services between Manchester Central and Guide Bridge consisted of seven trains (SX) in each direction. Saturday trains comprised six out of Manchester, but only five going into the city. Amazingly, the last of these was at 1.50pm from Guide Bridge. Sunday services had been withdrawn completely.

Coaching stock on the locals was comprised of a fascinating medley: some trains were formed of CLC stock which infilled between working over the Liverpool, Chester or Southport lines. It is worth noting that the CLC had their own route to Southport terminating in Lord Street station (closed 1952) and reached via the Southport Extension line. Indeed, up until 1958 Sunday excursion trains to the Lancashire seaside town (which rarely saw the sea!) were a regular feature from both Wilbraham Road and Fallowfield and were popular with the many local Sunday Schools. Other formations consisted of LNER suburban stock and some workings used main line vehicles (qv). At least one set of six-wheelers lasted well into the 1930s and has been captured on camera hauled by the impressive "Sir Sam Fay" 4-6-0, once the pride of the GCR.

But it was the local schools that provided much of the "commuter" traffic over the line in the years following the Second War. A number of established secondary schools were served by the stations, notably St.Bede's college in Alexandra Park, Chorlton High School and William Hulme's grammar school, all served by Wilbraham Road. Down the line at Fallowfield, the Hollies Convent grammar school for girls, the Manchester Grammar school for boys and the Manchester Girls' high school and Fallowfield Central girls' school were all within easy walking distance of the station. Fallowfield station was sited on the main Wilmslow Road while Wilbraham Road was only a short walk up from the same-named thoroughfare. Yet, despite the competing tram services – replaced by buses from 1938 – the local trains managed to hold on to at least some of their traffic. **Below: Typifying latter-day local workings, N5 No.E9343 approaches the station with the 6.04 pm from Guide Bridge on May 12th 1948. The first of the 5 coaches is an ex-GC clerestory brake composite designed to seat 10 first and 26 second class passengers. Would that today's commuters in "Nodding Donkeys" could enjoy such comfort!** ***J.D.Darby/Manchester Loco Society***

has been known to flood causing problems at Wilbraham Road station. A friend of the author's, Tony Quirke, related how on arrival for his trip home from nearby St.Bede's college to catch the 4.18 pm local to Guide Bridge he had to wait until the signalman operated the sluice gates behind the box and the water subsided from platform level. A far cry from modern times when an immediate line closure would almost certainly ensue followed by the ubiquitous "rail replacement" bus service!
Entering Fallowfield via a curve the alignment of the railway steepened, as mentioned elsewhere. A generous-sized goods yard was positioned on the line's south side. This handled mainly coal traffic, though in latter days the London Brick company established a depot here. The yard was accessed in the traditional fashion via trailing crossovers from both east and west ends. Conveniently placed, a signalbox in traditional MS&L style was positioned on the down platform. Leaving Fallowfield and travelling towards Levenshulme the railway cuts through red sandstone rock. Between 1907-1910 the GCR let contracts to for the excavation of sandstone at the back of the goods yard at Fallowfield and on the up side of the line east of the station to one, Mr.Barnes. The excavations must have been quite extensive: drawings show removal of rock to a depth of some 20 ft. Remains of the marks from this impromptu quarrying operation are still visible today.

FALLOWFIELD AND MANCHESTER (CENTRAL).

| | WEEK DAYS. | | | | | | | | | | | | | | | |
|---|---|---|---|---|---|---|---|---|---|---|---|---|---|---|---|---|
| | mrn | mrn | mrn | mrn | mrn | mrn | mrn | aft | aft | aft | aft | aft | aft | aft | aft | aft |
| FALLOWFIELD....dep. | 7 35 | 8 15 | 8 45 | 9 20 | 9 52 | 1032 | 1053 | 1239 | 1 4 | 1 28 | 1 44 | 2 19 | 3 49 | 4 15 | 5 8 | 6 13 |
| Chorlton ..........arr. | 7 43 | 8 22 | .... | .... | .... | 1039 | 11 0 | 1246 | 1 11 | 1 35 | 1 51 | .... | 3 56 | .... | .... | .... |
| MANCHESTER (C.) ,, | 7 52 | 8 31 | 8 57 | 9 32 | 10 4 | 1048 | 11 9 | 1255 | 1 20 | 1 44 | 2 0 | 2 31 | 4 5 | 4 27 | 5 20 | 6 25 |

| | WEEK DAYS—Continued. | | | | | | | | | | SUNDAYS. | | | | | |
|---|---|---|---|---|---|---|---|---|---|---|---|---|---|---|---|---|
| | aft | aft | aft | aft | aft | aft | aft | aft | | | mrn | aft | aft | aft | aft | |
| FALLOWFIELD....dep. | 6 40 | 7 18 | 7 39 | 8 4 | 9 4 | 9 25 | 10 5 | 1120 | .... | .... | 8 40 | 1 5 | 2 55 | 6 25 | 9 5 | .... |
| Chorlton ..........arr. | 6 46 | .... | 7 46 | 8 11 | 9 11 | .... | 1011 | 1126 | .... | .... | 8 46 | 1 11 | 3 1 | 6 31 | 9 11 | .... |
| MANCHESTER (C.) ,, | 6 55 | 7 30 | 7 55 | 8 20 | 9 20 | 9 37 | 1020 | 1135 | .... | .... | 8 55 | 1 20 | 3 10 | 6 40 | 9 20 | ... |

**Fallowfield station, late 1890s:** A charming Victorian scene showing the exterior of the station in all its MS&L finery. Reproduced from a contemporary postcard, the picture shows off the carefully-styled features and almost lavish details: stained glass windows, panelled doors, stone lintels, ornate gas lamps and the wonderful cast iron cupola – a feature of all the three roadside stations (Hyde Road being the exception). Admiring this scene we are transported back, not only in time by over a hundred and ten years or so, but to another world: one where a different social order prevailed. Over on the corner of Ladybarn Road and Wilmslow Road a lady with her child – adorned in typical Victorian middle-class attire, pauses to chat to a gentleman passer-by. To the right a second lady pushes her pram ("perambulator" back then) past the entrance to the *Great Central Goods & Mineral Depot.* Notice the tram rails inset in the cobbled roadway. Horse-drawn trams had arrived in Fallowfield in 1880; no overhead wires appear yet, the electric trams not arriving until December 1902. Thankfully this splendid building is still with is today, though the MS&L crest and attendant feature over the main doorway disappeared long ago. Now a Sainsbury's supermarket, Fallowfield station yet survives - in its third century of existence. *Author's collection*

**Fallowfield station, September 29th 1956:** "Hard at it" and ready for the bank up to Levenshulme is B1 No.61161, the one-time favourite and charge of Gorton driver Arthur Orsler. The train is the Liverpool-Hull express, one of the two "Boat" trains that were daily fare over the Fallowfield line up to the early 1960s. The B1 will only travel as far as Guide Bridge where, dare we mention it, electric traction will take over as far as Sheffield Victoria. Details abound in this lovely sunny view: the neat little plantings of flowers round the base of the lamp posts; these were a special delight on the line's stations – with a "tulip-shaped" base and topped originally by a square glass lantern through which the delicate yellow gas flame shone, the station's name shining etched on the glass and glowing in the dark. Sainsbury's car park just doesn't cut it somehow!

*Neville Fields/Manchester Loco Society*

**Fallowfield station, April 2nd 1951:** Gorton's N5 No.69353 waits for the Up Home signal with a train of wagon empties. Woodhead was as much about coal traffic as anything else and these wooden-bodied specimens must have "trodden the boards" many thousands of times through the infamous tunnel. Freight traffic around Manchester was both intense and complex in the years after the Second war. Guide Bridge, Dewsnap sidings, Ashburys and Ardwick were all busy centres for traffic handling and the train here could be bound for any of these. Prominent above the loco is the water tank provided for the Fallowfield banker referred to elsewhere. Notice the somewhat dilapidated state of the platform canopies, though the end screens are still in place. The platform-mounted signalbox was a special delight retaining its GC wooden-cased block instruments until well into the 1960s.

*Neville Fields/Manchester Loco Society*

**Fallowfield station, n.d:** Photographs taken on the Fallowfield line in the pre-Group era are, to say the least, rare. So it is with great pleasure that I am including this picture. Waiting for the Home signal at the end of the Up platform is Class 8B Atlantic No.1092, a North British Loco Co. product of November 1905. Running light engine the loco may well be on a running-in or "Trials" trip from Gorton works. Looking spotless and adorned in the GCR's dark green passenger livery, lined black and white and with vermillion splasher panels bearing the company's coat of arms, this was, to be sure, Edwardian elegance at its finest. No.1092 was renumbered 6092 under the LNER, becoming No.2915. It was withdrawn in June 1949.

*Collection of Norman Spilsbury*

**Fallowfield station, c.1927:** One of the most significant events concerning express passenger workings over the line was the introduction of through loco working from Manchester to Ipswich in 1927. This brought, initially, the former GER B12 4-6-0s, followed by the B17s to the railway. Geoff Platt had but a box camera when he caught this example: a B12 running through Fallowfield with the Up "Continental". Though of poor quality, the photograph remains as one of just three known examples of these ground-breaking workings.

*G.H.Platt*

**Fallowfield station, c.1944:** The bland initials "NE" on the loco's tender betray a wartime view as B7 No.5475 enters the station with a Down express. Doubtless, Bill Lees' press credentials gave him a certain amount of freedom with his camera, something that was denied to the general public. Wartime regulations imposed restrictions on the photography of the nation's transport infrastructure; even note-taking could be viewed with suspicion! *William Lees*

(887)

MANCHESTER,
SHEFFIELD, and LINCOLNSHIRE
RAILWAY.

On Thursday, October 1st,
THE
NEW LINE
BETWEEN
MANCHESTER (Central)
AND
FALLOWFIELD

*Will be opened for Passenger Traffic, and Trains will run as shown on the other side.*

WILLIAM POLLITT,
General Manager.

*London Road Station, Manchester.*

**Fallowfield goods yard, c.June/July 1917:** The spacious goods yard at Fallowfield served as a backdrop for several superb pictures of Great Central locomotives. Ample room, coupled with easy reach of Gorton and access from both east and west ends may well have been the reasons. The noted photographer P.F.Cooke of Huddersfield took pictures here, although it is not known if he was behind the camera on this occasion. No.371 was outshopped from Gorton works on June 30th 1917, one of J.G.Robinson's very successful Class 9N (LNE A5) 4-6-2 tank engines which had first appeared in 1911. No.371 was one of a third batch: five locomotives produced by the GCR between June and October 1917. Another ten appeared under LNER jurisdiction in 1923 with a final clutch of thirteen locos – with some minor modifications - being built by Hawthorn, Leslie & Co. in 1925/26. Looking in absolutely "mint" condition, No.371 stands alongside the Down line. The crew are posing obligingly for the photographer and the station's large goods shed forms a fine background. As mentioned elsewhere, the A5s were firm favourites over the Fallowfield line in the BR era prior to 1958 being regular performers with the Harwich and Hull boat trains between Manchester Central and Guide Bridge. No.371 ended its days as BR No.69815 and was withdrawn in July 1957. *Collection of J.Suter*

**(Opposite) Fallowfield signalbox late 1960s**: A touch of modernisation shows in the shape of BR standard block instruments seen above the RSC-pattern frame. Track circuit lights show up on the paper diagram and electric locking was in place on the Up and Down Starting signals. A 26-lever RSC frame was provided, originally there were 18 working levers, but these have now been reduced – the west crossover and siding access having been removed; notice the white-painted levers on the left-hand side. Fond memories of a visit here in Jume 1961 recall an instructional evening with relief signalman "Trevor" (surname not recorded). GC-pattern wooden-cased block instruments were still in use back then. Two final touches of antiquity: the enamel water jug by the window – no running water – and the gas lamp – no mains electricity either! *Graham Vickers*

## Up the bank towards Levenshulme

Forward and on up the bank towards Levenshulme the railway encountered the first of three lines to cross its path as it passed beneath the LNWR's "Styal Line" – the Wilmslow & Levenshulme Railway – opened from Slade Lane Junction on the Manchester to Stockport line in 1909 and re-joining the latter just south of Wilmslow in Cheshire. Just over ½ mile further east the Fallowfield line passed beneath the Stockport line itself via what was effectively a small tunnel, the line above having been widened to four tracks in the mid-1880s. Then, passing beneath the Stockport Road (A6) the railway encountered Levenshulme station – always "Levenzoom" to the local inhabitants. The station was re-named "Levenshulme South" in September 1952 to distinguish it from its LNWR neighbour sited just north, off the A6. When the line was built two signalboxes were provided here; one controlled the goods yard; the other – a mere 448 yards away - served the station

Going east from Levenshulme the railway passed through a changed landscape, one scarred by clay pits and small reservoirs. Over many years local brick-makers, notably Messrs.J & A Jackson, were active in working out the clay deposits. The land at the back of the down line, beyond Levenshulme station, was worked extensively right up until modern times and a brick works was sited on Broom Avenue, close to the railway. Possibly, it was with these clay workings in mind that a proposal for a second yard at Levenshulme was made. Drawings dated February 1908 show seven extra roads plus a shunting neck on the line's down side opposite the existing yard. The new sidings would have held 211 wagons as well as 22 in the neck; but, in the event, the proposals were never fulfilled. One of Levenshulme's other local industries was the famed UCP tripe works. This sat aside a passage that led along the north side of the goods yard and could be seen clearly from the signalbox. A large concern – there was a big demand for "cattle products" in Lancashire at one time – activity at the works was shown by a large chimney which constantly emitted steam, presumably from the boilers that cooked such delicacies as cows' heels! No rail traffic emanated from the UCP factory, nor from Levenshulme's various industries: the Highfield iron works, the adjacent carpet factory and the bleach and dye works which stood beyond the brick works by the side of High Field Farm. More clay workings existed further east along the line towards Reddish and Hyde Road and a small set of sidings was installed between Levenshulme and Hyde Road to serve a second brick works. Controlled by a small signalbox known as "Brick Kiln Siding" (closed 1906), the set of six sidings lay on the down side of the line just over 1 mile north-east of Levenshulme station. A small extension fed another local concern, the Climax Engineering Works. Opened by 1897 the provision was short-lived; the archives of the Railway Signalling Company record that Brick Kiln Siding box was closed on January 29th 1906. It was opposite this site that the Reddish Electric Depot was later built.

**Between Fallowfield and Levenshulme, early 1950s:** An unidentified K3 pounds up the 1-in-100 bank towards Levenshulme with a 6-coach express, The photographer is stood on the overbridge carrying the LNWR's Styal line from Slade Lane Junction to Wilmslow. A small piece of social history unfolds as we look at the ramshackle housebacks of the terraces along neighbouring Moseley Road in Fallowfield. Huts, chicken sheds and all manner of things abound behind the houses; this was post-War austerity Britain when resourcefulness was still the watchword. *Alan Newton*

## Main line services post-Grouping

In the period up to Grouping the pattern of main line services remained similar to those pertaining prior to WWI. Main line departures over the Fallowfield line from Manchester Central just prior to Grouping comprised the Harwich Boat train, the so-called "North Country Continental", the expresses to Hull and the Sundays Only 12.15 pm express to London Marylebone, due in the Capital at 5.45 pm. Come evening and arriving into Manchester Central at 7.25 pm was an express, the so-called Sheffield Special. A restaurant car train introduced by the GCR in 1903, the service ran non-stop from Marylebone to Sheffield in a time of 3 hours, 8 minutes, later 2 hours, 50 minutes. A lightweight train of only three, later five, coaches – The Sheffield Special slipped one coach (a non-corridor) at Leicester - for Grimsby and Cleethorpes - and a second at Penistone - for Bradford. Stopping then only at Guide Bridge, the train arrived in Central in time to connect with the 7.30 express to Liverpool. Originally the province of the Robinson D9 4-4-0s the train was taken over by the Robinson "Atlantics", then the "Directors". In LNER days, from the early 1930s, B17s were used on the London expresses. No corresponding weekday up trains departing Manchester Central appeared in LNER timetables, the GC and LNE retaining their use of London Road for these services and referred to in the London Road feature.

Returning to Manchester, arrivals at Central were at 11.09 am (8.20 ex Leicester), while 6.02 in the evening saw the arrival of an express from Hull – again, reversing before going on to Liverpool, while at 7.20 the through carriages from Bournemouth (departing at 10.47 am) rolled into the terminus.

With the cessation of the Gorton lodging turns from 1941 the through loco workings disappeared. After nationalisation "The Continental" had a spell of working from Parkeston to Lincoln by a Parkeston B1; here an Immingham D10 or D11 worked the train forward to Sheffield. In the autumn of 1949, following the removal of the D10s from Immingham, K3s from that shed took over working of the train. At this time former Southern Railway Bulleid Tavern cars appeared on "The Continental" along with an SR restaurant car. Interestingly, back in the nineteenth century, the celebrated cross-country train had been amongst the first in the country to be afforded restaurant car facilities.

## Other express workings over the Fallowfield line

The Great Northern's right of access into Manchester has already been touched on. But when the Great Central (MS&L up to August 1st 1897) opened their London Extension on March 15th 1899, the GNR, newly flexing their muscles in the area via their magnificent new goods warehouse at Deansgate in Manchester city centre, took over the running of the expresses to King's Cross from Manchester. By no means a new thing: the MS&L, in concert with the GN, had been running these joint express services from Manchester London Road to King's Cross from as far back as August 1857. Travelling via Woodhead and thence the GN main line, engines had been changes first at Retford and later, at Grantham. But now, from March1899, the GN were firmly in charge throughout. Initially five trains each way were tried and all bar one travelled via Fallowfield (the last train of the day – at 11.05 pm – travelled over the South District line and then via Stockport Tiviot Dale). GN Class D2 (LNER D3) 4-4-0s were used on the services. Newly-built, six of the 4-4-0s were allocated to Trafford Park to take over the new passenger workings, though the engines were also used on some express goods trains from Deansgate. Trains were light: Rous-Marten had sampled the service and noted that three bogie coaches, plus two 12-wheel dining cars made up the formation. His train had been hauled over the section of the journey from King's Cross to Nottingham by a Stirling 8-footer. In 1906 the GN introduced new luxury trains for its Manchester services – the stock having been designed by the company's newly-appointed carriage and wagon superintendent, H.N.Gresley. But even these trains were not a match for the competing GC, LNW and Midland services, the latter now in an improved position due to the opening of the 1902 high speed cut-off line via Heaton Mersey and New Mills South Junction. The GN's star in Manchester soon began to fall and by July 1907 non-stop running from Sheffield to London had ceased. GN trains through Fallowfield were no more after this time; the remaining King's Cross trains being routed back to London Road.

In the meantime, from the turn of the century, the GCR began to transfer some of their express services over from London Road to Manchester Central. Within three years morning departures from Central were at 9.20 - with through coaches for Oxford, Southampton and Bournemouth, the train having begun from Liverpool at 8.30. At 10.20 was an express for Hull, another Liverpool starter. Moving to evening and at 7.20 for Leicester (Central) followed by the overnight newspaper and mail to Marylebone at 10.30 pm. Though not officially a passenger train as such, the 10.30 carried two coaches and was due into Marylebone at 4.20 in the morning.

## Football excursions

Before the days of universal car ownership, travel to football matches was a major source of traffic for the railways. One football ground that experienced large attendances was the former home ground of Manchester City at Maine Road. City's rivals at Old Trafford had the luxury of a dedicated station on the CLC's Liverpool line which had opened in 1936. Manchester City, however, had to make do with Fallowfield, a good mile way as the crow flies and to where such traffic had been running since 1924. Notes made by Brian Green dated March 27th 1954 show no less than ten specials arriving variously from Sheffield, Retford and Ollerton (near Mansfield) for the FA cup semi-final between Sheffield Wednesday and Preston North End. Seven of the specials arrived at Manchester London Road while three trains left Sheffield Victoria that day for Fallowfield: at 10.45 am hauled by V2 No.60896 with 10 coaches; at 11.50 with B1 No.61183 (39B) with 10 coaches and at 12.25 pm with B1 61283 (38A) hauling 9 coaches. The fans' empty stock would have been berthed for the afternoon (kick-off was at 3 o'clock) in Cornbrook carriage sidings with the locos sojourning at Trafford Park. Alas for the Wednesday fans they must have returned home dejected; their team lost 2-0 to Preston. For the record, Preston met West Brom at Wembley for the Final on May 1st with the Brummies winning the Cup 3-2!

**RIGHT:** Two sturdy GCR signals, always fascinating for both enthusiast and modeller. **(Top) August 10th 1954:** The Levenshulme Up Distant; sited just behind Kingsway this lower quadrant specimen lasted until around 1957 until replacement with an upper quadrant. At around 1500 yards from the box, a hefty pull was needed! **(Bottom) March 27th 1950:** This lofty signal with co-acting arms was the Levenshulme Up Home signal. In front is bridge No.19 carrying the LNWR's Manchester London Road to Crewe line over the railway here. Almost a short tunnel, the bridge carried the four-track main line as well as the sidings at Levenshulme LNW (later "North") station. *R.E.Gee*

**Levenshulme 1949:** Gorton's B1 No.61182 storms into the station and heads along towards Hyde Road with an Up Hull express. A Vulcan Foundry engine, built in 1947 No.61182 looks resplendent in fresh black paint, the "BRITISH RAILWAYS" lettering showing clearly on the tender. Notice the plain "LEVENSHULME" on the LNER's station nameboard on concrete posts just behind one of those wonderful MS&L gas lamps. Just visible through the cloud of steam is the fine glazed footbridge and the roof-mounted cupola similar that of its neighbours down the line. To the side is Station Road, re-named today as "Crayfield Road".
*Neville Fields/Manchester Loco Society*

**Levenshulme South, October 10th 1954:** Now with a "handle" to its name, the station's quiet is shattered by the sound of A5 tank No.69817 pulling up the bank with one of the "Boat Trains" bound for either Harwich or Hull. An odd working over the line was the 9.25 am Hull express; this called at Fallowfield, a practice dating back to the time before WWI. This view at Levenshulme, presenting a wider perspective, shows clearly the spacious nature of the Fallowfield line's stations; all built, sadly, for a purpose never fulfilled. *Neville Fields/Manchester Loco Society*

## Seasonal trains

Away from the congested approaches in and out of Manchester's London Road station over the former GC main line, the Fallowfield line was well-suited for some occasional extra traffic. This was comprised mostly of Saturdays only seaside trains to the East Coast resorts. Notes made by the late David Swift for the summer of 1938 show a good variety of such traffic – working out of Manchester Central and using the line. The morning period: 8.20 to Noon saw five trains: one each to Skegness, Clacton, Scarborough and two to Yarmouth. 2.53 pm saw an SO express to Cambridge; a relief train to the 3.10 pm. An ex-works B17 was noted as hauling this train on occasions. A second afternoon special turned up in the shape of an MFSO express to Cleethorpes. Leaving Central at 3.20 this train conveyed a through coach from Liverpool. Another special worthy of note, this time working in to Manchester Central was the Fridays-only express from Immingham. Run in conjunction with the Orient Shipping Company's Norwegian cruises and dubbed "Orient Express" by local enthusiasts, the train – numbered S255 – was often a B7 duty. Seasonal passenger traffic continued to modern times: well remembered is a Saturday morning - August 5th 1961 - the Bank Holiday weekend, with train after train passing the signalbox at Levenshulme towards Hyde Road Junction in a seemingly never-ending procession.

**LEFT:** The signalbox at Levenshulme South seen in September 1961. Originally known as "Levenshulme Goods" it was one of two signalboxes here; the second being at the east end of the Down platform. The brick base was untypically MS&L/GC for this area; the majority of boxes being all-timber. *Author*

**Levenshulme, March 18th 1949:** Former GC Class 8G (B9) No.61475 passes Levenshulme signalbox with a Halewood (Liverpool) to Dewsnap freight. The front portion of the train consists of five petrol tankers; notice the van required under regulations to be marshalled between the flammable load and the locomotive. No.61475 was a Beyer, Peacock & Co. product of 1906. As LNE No.6111 the loco was withdrawn in July 1939 only to be restored to traffic two months later. She was withdrawn eventually in May 1949, the last survivor of the class. *J.D.Darby/Manchester Loco Society*

## Characters along the line

Well remembered by the writer were the three signalmen at Levenshulme South in the summer of 1961. Ernie Thompson had started his railway career as a booking lad in the former GC power box at Manchester's London Road (now Piccadilly) station. Levenshulme (a Class 4 position) was his first solo box and he later moved to Ashton Moss South Junction - a Class 3 post with higher pay. Signalmen were poorly paid in those days: the basic rate for a 40-hour week being just under £9.00. His fellow signalmen were Gerry Spinetto and Jack Boon. Jack had worked at Levenshulme pretty well all his life - from around some time before the First War. I remember him as a somewhat taciturn man with a rather grumpy disposition. Another popular character was Charlie Minch, a permanent way patrol man whose domain extended from Hyde Road as far as the Fallowfield down distant signal. Along the line at Wilbraham Road signalbox one, Jack William Smith, seems to be the earliest recorded signalman – known to and photographed by G.H. Platt as far back as 1927. In 1932 we find Jack sharing signalling duties at Wilbraham Road with two other men: Henry Dowling and Henry Charles Houghton.

## A look back at pay and conditions

Pity poor Smith and his colleagues in those far-off days. Looking at his wage record card for 1932/33 we see him earning a basic wage of £2/13/3d for a 48-hour week. In the week ending January 14th 1933 Jack Smith fell ill for three days and received a mere £1/6/10d. Returning to work the following week saw him take home full pay (£2/17/7d); but, alas, the following week Jack fell ill again and received no pay at all.

The history of these parlous wages of the railwaymen of around eighty years ago is worth a mention. Under a National Agreement of 1920 railwaymen's pay had been set at a guaranteed minimum rate. For signalmen this ranged from 46/- to 70/- per week. Although a further improvement came in 1922 with a new marks system for signalmen's classifications; starting from August 13th 1929 wages were reduced overall by 2½%. Though the impost was removed just under a year later, in March 1931 the 2½% cut was re-imposed and worse still - at the same time - the National Wages Board ordered a further 2½% to be docked from the amount by which wages exceeded 40/- per week. It was not until August 1937 that pay was restored fully to the levels of the 1920s. A reflection on what were harsh times indeed and something that should make us realise just how far pay and working conditions have improved since then. Referring back briefly to the 1930 RAS show. Tow years later, the LNER were still employing a cattle wagon cleaner at Wilbraham Road. The post was held by John Edward Gould. Paid £2/2/10d per week (some 11 shillings less than his signalmen colleagues here) poor John had to travel daily from Heaton Chapel, Stockport, to perform what must have been one of the most unpleasant jobs on the railway.

Slightly later on, Alban Daley, along with Jack Smith, was one of the box's occupants with Ronnie Gee who worked there (as well as at Levenshulme) in the years following the Second war. Up the line at Fallowfield William Cunnington was to be Fallowfield's last stationmaster. Under the heading *"No more noise, no more bustle"* he appeared in a feature in the Manchester Evening News in July1959, a full year after the local trains finished and the station had closed to passengers (July 5th. 1958). Little could Cunnington know that, fifty years later, his station would have been turned into half supermarket and half-pub, all creating a great deal more noise and bustle than his station ever did! William Cunnington had been appointed Stationmaster at Fallowfield in 1948; he retired to Worksop where he began his railway career at the age of 15.

**Levenshulme South, July 1961:** Characters along the line..... Ernie Thompson pictured at work pulling over lever No.9 - "EAST CROSSOVER - MAIN- CROSSOVER". Of particular interest is the fine lever description board behind the GC-pattern frame. Floridly adorned and lettered "G.C.R," it has fortunately survived and can be seen today in the refreshment rooms at Stalybridge station. Notice the BR block instruments and the illumnated panel showing the track layout and track circuits. Though such modernisation had come late to Levenshulme, the box was without running water, mains electricity or sanitation; the latter relying on an "Elsan" toilet cupboard outside the box. For those signalmen who preferred modernity in the toilet department, the station toilets, despite closure some thre years earlier, were but a short walk down the track! Electric lighting was "illegally" obtained from a connection to the track circuit panel at the rear of the box. A curiosity (at least to the author) was the bank of Leclanché cells behind the box. This was the "backup" provided in the event of track circuit failure. Though such malfunctions were rare, there was the odd occasion when the Down Starter (a colour light) failed, something that was indicated via a lamp below the block shelf. Trains were accepted in the normal way, but the Distant signal was left "on" , the signalman then leant out of the box window holdong a red flag. Instructions were shouted to the driver to "pass the Starter at danger - signal failure!" Crude, maybe, but it all worked in perfect safety. *Author*

**Onwards towards Hyde Road**

Hyde Road differed from its neighbours down the line in being in an elevated position, sited on an embankment and reached via stairs from the Hyde Road (A57) that passed beneath the railway. The platform buildings, of brick with attractive decorative inlays, had a single gable at each end presenting a somewhat different appearance from the other stations down the line. Economy-minded, though strange on this railway, the Up platform was built from wood. Early references refer to "Reservoir Station"; likewise, the adjacent junction was referred to as "Reservoir Junction." (Allusions to the two adjacent large reservoirs belonging to Manchester Corporation).The suffix "for Belle Vue" was, to be sure, more than a trifle disingenuous. Passengers alighting at Hyde Road were faced with an almost one mile walk back down the A57 and a further three-quarters of a mile or so down Kirkmanshulme Lane to reach Belle Vue itself, once the entertainment mecca of the North-West. But perhaps pre-1958 passengers, not being car-reliant, were less fazed by such a long walk! For such hardy souls the MS&L had provided an excursion platform: consisting of an island it was serviced by two dead end siding roads. Another attraction, the beautiful and spacious Debdale Park, was a mere stone's throw from Hyde Road station. A third siding was sited behind the excursion platforms; while a fourth siding stretched down towards the Stockport branch of the Ashton Canal close to where a wharf was sited serving the Tan Yard Foundry Mill.

**Hyde Road station, September 11th 1953:** All wired and ready to go, though the canopies have been removed to improve clearance for the OHL. Looking at today's gridlocked A57 one cannot but wonder why such a suburban station and electrically-serviced at that, could not have had a better future. Maybe even as part of an expanded Metrolink?
*Oliver Carter*

**Hyde Road station, c.1950:** Seen from the signalbox B1 No.61214, a foreigner to these parts – from Stockton – clears the station with an Up fitted freight. How neat and attractive the station looks; notice the canopies have yet to be removed. Two interesting-looking vans inhabit the goods yard, sadly the quality of the picture inhibits any positive identification.
*Neville Fields/ Manchester Loco Society*

## Hyde Road Junction

In like manner to its counterpart station, the junction – dividing point for the northerly fork to Gorton and the north-easterly fork to Fairfield – began life as "Reservoir Junction". An early MS&L line plan shows the first signalbox here tucked into the fork of the junction, just above a footpath that led from High Bank (north of Hyde Road) across to a second path leading from Greenfold down to the Gorton lower reservoir on the fringe of Debdale Park. This first box had a only a short life, being closed on January 29th 1906. A sectional appendix shows the box then as controlling Fairfield goods yard and listed as "ex Hyde Road Junction". A second signalbox at Hyde Road was sited at the station; this, too, was short-lived and closed at the same time as its junction neighbour. Signalling operations from both boxes were taken over by the new Hyde Road junction box in January 1906. This later box controlled the sections to Levenshulme, to Gorton station and to Fairfield junction; from 1954 Hyde Road Junction box also controlled movements in and out of the Reddish electric Depot.

**Hyde Road signalbox, June 2nd 1977:** Looking pristine and bathed in sunlight the signalbox bears all the hallmarks of MS&L/GCR design: lapped and boarded woodwork with the very familiar fretted bargeboards and substantial wooden finials at the gable ends. The detached chemical toilet is *not* a GCR artefact! The Railway Signalling Company's frame housed 36 levers of which 30 were working with 6 spare levers. Rationalisation took place in 1971 when the station sidings were taken out of use and the frame reduced to 21 working levers. This was commensurate with the closure of the signalboxes at Levenshulme South and Fallowfield. Hyde Road Junction lasted until the closure of the Fallowfield line, sending its final 7 pause 5 pause 5 on October 15th 1988. The box was subsequently destroyed by fire. *Raymond Keeley*

**Hyde Road Junction on July 26th 1952:** Typifying summer excursion traffic over Woodhead via the Fallowfield line is this shot: a late evening picture showing an unidentified J39 0-6-0 at the head of the Saturdays only Mablethorpe to Manchester Central dropping down from Fairfield junction. Hyde Road junction box can be seen to the left; notice the signal is "off" for the curve round to Fairfield. To the right the Pennine hills form a backdrop to the reservoirs on the fringe of nearby Debdale Park. The overhead structures have yet to acquire their catenary for the forthcoming MSW scheme – the full implementation of which might have saved this once-important line. *R.E.Gee*

**Fairfield, September 9th 1950:** Gorton's K3 No.61829 storms through the Up Fallowfield line platform with the Saturdays only morning express from Manchester Central to Yarmouth. Departing at 8.42 from Central's platform 5 the loco left Gorton at 7.40. The coaching stock originated from Cornbrook carriage sidings. *Neville Fields/Manchester Loco Society*

**Fairfield, September 8th 1951:** N5 0-6-2 tank No.69370 awaits departure with the 12.00 Manchester Central to Guide Bridge stopping train. Passing through Fairfield today it is almost impossible to imagine scenes such as these: full passenger facilities, four main running lines, a branch passenger service and six platforms to boot. *Neville Fields/Manchester Loco Society*

## Impact of electrification

Though this volume is essentially about the steam era over Woodhead it is pertinent to recall some staple facts concerning the transition from steam to electric traction and how this impinged on the latter days of steam traction over Woodhead. Before the transfer of the ex-GCR lines west of Woodhead to the LMR in February 1958, B1s had become staple motive power for the Harwich and Hull boat trains from Sheffield Victoria into Manchester Central. But all was to change from September 1954 when the MSW (Manchester-Sheffield-Wath) lines were fully electrified. Using the 1,500V dc system, the scheme had been hatched by the LNER in 1936 but had been all but postponed with the onset of the Second War. When work resumed in 1946 it was found necessary to replace the original twin brick-lined Woodhead tunnels with a new single bore lined with concrete. The original MSW scheme allowed for the whole of the system from Sheffield into Manchester to be electrified and this would have included the Fallowfield line and the connecting line from Chorlton Junction into Manchester Central. Sadly, due to the expenditure required for the new tunnel – £2.3M – the scheme had to be cut back and the overhead line never got beyond Reddish. It was here that a new maintenance and repair depot for the MSW electric locomotives and EMUs was built. Erected on land that had formerly housed a reservoir, the depot opened in the summer of 1954.

Reddish depot had a secondary claim to fame that has been little recorded. When the *Midland Pullman* high-speed DMU was introduced to the Manchester Central-St.Pancras route on July 4th 1960 the two 6-car train sets were stabled and maintained at the depot. Returning at night, around 10.15 as ECS, the train presented an eerie sight purring through the darkness with all lights in the passenger cars extinguished. Train diagrams were different in those days: the *Midland Pullman* sets ran a fortnight at a time (Mondays-Fridays only), during which period the "spare" set was out of traffic undergoing servicing at Reddish. Interestingly, the first time a Pullman train was recorded on the Fallowfield line was in the period April to September 1925 when the short-lived *Sheffield & Manchester Pullman* running non-stop from King's Cross to Sheffield via Retford, was tried. A final footnote concerning electric traction over Woodhead and involving the Fallowfield line is worthy of a mention. Despite closure on July 7th 1958 Hyde Road stations platforms remained intact. On Monday April 18th 1960 (Easter Monday) the platforms here were re-opened and used by two excursions to Belle Vue. These were from Thorne South and Kirkby Bentinck, returning from Hyde Road at 9.17 pm and 9.26 pm respectively. Both specials were electrically-hauled from Sheffield Victoria, the locos then taking the empty coaches on to Reddish depot. Thus was provided the only known spectacle of an electrically-hauled passenger train over part of the Fallowfield line.

So with no overhead line into Manchester Central, all through electrically-hauled passenger trains from Sheffield down the Fallowfield line had to undergo an engine change at Guide Bridge (though there is some evidence that this was done on occasions at Godley Junction). Initially the work was the province of Gorton A5 4-6-2 tanks, the occasional K3 Moguls and Thompson L1 2-6-4 tanks. The locos would work light engine to and from Gorton shed, filling in with ECS turns from Central to Ardwick carriage sidings. After the LM region took over the former LNER lines west of the Pennines from April 1958, "Crab" 2-6-0s appeared on the daily pilots at Hyde Road, Levenshulme South and Fallowfield. The same locos appeared on the Central-Guide Bridge leg of the Harwich and Hull boat trains before and after these were handed over to electric traction from Guide Bridge to Sheffield Victoria. Stanier 2-6-4 tanks were also seen on these duties in this period. Such locomotives looked strange to those enthusiasts who, for many years, had become accustomed to the sight and sound of the big A5 tanks heaving their way up the bank through Fallowfield with their set of Gresley coaches in the familiar "blood and custard" beloved of early period British Railways. The A5s seemed popular with Gorton crews, with one member remarking: "those engines could easily have taken the train right through to Sheffield!"

## The final years

Though the Fallowfield line did not feature on Beeching's agenda, British Railways had their own ideas for the future of South Manchester's railways. After full electrification of the ex-LNWR Manchester-London route via Crewe and Stoke both the ex-GC line from Sheffield to Marylebone and the Midland route via Peak Forest through Cheadle Heath into Manchester Central were listed for closure. As mentioned previously, local services over the Fallowfield line had finished in the summer of 1958 and those on the adjacent ex-Midland South District line were then a dead letter as well, there being no PTE in existence to acknowledge "social need" and subsidise loss-making local lines. Manchester Central station closed in May 1969, its local and Liverpool services transferred to Oxford Road and main line services – principally the St.Pancras expresses and the Harwich boat trains, transferred from 1963 to Manchester Piccadilly. Now the Fallowfield line had lost its remaining through expresses, the locals were long gone and, by the mid-1960s, the local goods trains – mainly comprised of coal traffic – were finished as well, a victim of the various clean air acts. Fallowfield experienced a brief resurgence in freight handling in the 1970s when the London Brick Company used the sidings for their traffic, something substantial enough to warrant the appointment of a site manager with operations lasting until 1984. Despite the Beeching closures BR were still being forced to rationalise some lines and programme that resulted in the Fallowfield line being reduced to single-track status between Old Trafford and Levenshulme in June 1974, to be followed by the section between Levenshulme and Hyde Road ten years later. The junction at Hyde Road disappeared w.e.f.September 14th 1983.At Wilbraham Road a substantial depot for the handling of bulk frozen food traffic with the SPD frozen food combine had been built on the large goods yard, the concern being given a 99-year lease by BR from May 4th 1961. Ultimately though, this traffic, too, ceased and the depot was demolished; a small housing estate now covers the site. The adjacent station buildings along Alexandra Road lasted into the early 1960s, surviving an arson attack. A few years later and the platform buildings there were bereft of glass and stood, skeleton-like, a sad reminder of former days.

## Blues and Gospel at Wilbraham Road

What must surely have been one of the strangest uses for a closed railway station occurred on Thursday May 7th 1964 when Manchester-based Granada TV turned Wilbraham Road into an impromptu theatre, giving it the name "Chorltonville". The occasion was for a show entitled "Blues and Gospel Train". Driven by Frankie Williamson with Fireman Tommy Jackson, the train of BR Mk I coaches began its journey at Manchester Central. It was hauled by an Ivatt Mogul loaned from Newton Heath and suitably mocked-up "American-style" at Trafford Park shed bearing the legend on the smokebox door – HALLELUJAH! The youthful audience were filmed eagerly leaping off the train and heading straight into their seats consisting of wooden planks and scaffolding poles on the up platform. Well-known jazz musicians were featured, including the legendary Sister Rosetta Tharpe along with Brownie McGee, Cousin Joe Pleasants, Sonny Terry and Muddy Waters. The platform buildings were spruced-up, with window shutters, barrels and carts added for American atmosphere; Sister Rosetta Tharpe was even filmed arriving on the down platform on a horse and cart. Her rendering of "Didn't it Rain" was accompanied by a typical Manchester cloudburst with accompanying gusts of wind! Directed by Granada's John Hamp, a clip can be seen on YouTube.

**Above:** Sister Rosetta Tharpe and others at "Chorltonville".-"Didn't it Rain!"

## Closure of the line

By the late 1970s only the afternoon Freightliner train from Trafford Park to Holyhead was the line's regular user. On Sunday, October 10th 1988 the last passenger train passed over the railway: this was a morning Sheffield-Liverpool train (09.09 ex Stockport Edgeley). Diverted over the Heaton Norris & Guide Bridge line the train used the erstwhile Throstle Nest curve to avoid both Piccadilly and Oxford Road stations where re-modelling and re-signalling were being carried out in connection with the new Manchester South signalling scheme. The end came the following Saturday, October 15th, when the 15.54 Freightliner from Trafford Park to Holyhead with Newton Heath driver Peter Drinkwater at the controls passed over the Fallowfield Line in the up direction. Now the line fell silent after some 96 years of traffic. Slowly, nature began to reclaim her once-violated territory; quickly the blackberry brambles encroached over the rusting single line and a multitude of sundry bushes and trees began to sprout. Track lifting began in September 1991 and was completed by around the end of the following year. Only the remains of the surplus ballast were left to serve as a reminder that there was once a railway here.

## The line today

At Wilbraham Road all traces of the station buildings have long gone, though the platform foundations remain. Along the line at Fallowfield, where the booking hall and offices had survived two attacks by arsonists, there had been for some years housed an eclectic mix of premises: estate agents, wine bar, off-licence and a delicatessen. After years of dereliction the whole site was bought by Sainsbury's to become a supermarket. Opened for business in 2000, the former goods yard has become Sainsbury's car park and room has been found for a small block of flats as well as a pub on the corner of Wilmslow Road and Ladybarn Road. In 1992, to their great credit, Railtrack completely refurbished Levenshulme's station buildings along the Stockport Road and thus Levenshulme station has survived to see their third century, though nothing of the platforms remain. The sidings east of the station were lifted in the 1980s and a pub, entitled "The Sidings" (what else?!), along with a small housing development along Pullman Close covers the ground. Over on the opposite side of the line the land once forming the clay pits for the brickworks of Messrs.Jackson has been infilled and landscaped to become "Highfield Country Park". Reddish Depot, closed in 1981, lingered for years before being demolished completely by BR in the mid-1990s. The site has now become a housing development. Of the Fallowfield line's four stations, Hyde Road has suffered the worst with not a vestige of the station buildings or platforms remaining today. Fairfield station, though still open today has, of course, lost its Fallowfield line platforms. Once boasting no less than six platforms, a mere two remain nowadays.

However, the section of line from Hyde Road Junction alongside Reddish depot was to have one little taste of suburban electrification. This came about for six days from Sunday March 22nd 1987 when the GMPTE was engaged in what was termed "Project Light Rail". Using a converted Docklands Light Railway EMU temporarily fitted with a pantograph, the unit ran up and down from a temporary wooden platform erected close to Debdale Park treating VIPs and visitors to a foretaste of what was then referred to as "LRT." Light Rail Transit were the contemporary buzzwords for the long-awaited solution enabling a cross-city rail link from Piccadilly to Victoria stations; a thing born after many years of fruitless planning which even involved a much-vaulted Underground system. The LRT theme finally bore fruit when, on July 17th 1992, Her Majesty the Queen officially opened Metrolink, the tram system that provided a link between Altrincham and Bury via Manchester Victoria and with a spur into Piccadilly station as well.

## The future

On April 28th 2002 the line was, to some extent, re-born when Sustrans – a national charity dedicated to converting derelict railway lines into cycle and walkways – opened what has become known as "The Fallowfield Loop". Stretching from Chorlton through to Debdale Park, just short of Fairfield, this is sponsored by its own "Friends" group and the author is pleased to have been involved. Beginning on October 4th 2008 reclamation of the trackbed from Old Trafford to Chorlton Junction – part of the erstwhile CLC route from Manchester Central – was begun. A Herculean task to enable an extension of Manchester's popular "Metrolink" tramway system from Old Trafford via Chorlton to East Didsbury and, ultimately, Manchester Airport. The initial part of the system, to St.Werburgh's Road – the site of the former Chorlton Junction – was opened on July 7th 2011. At the time of writing (May 2013) the opening of the extension along to East Didsbury, using part of the former Midland's Manchester South District Railway, is scheduled to enter service on May 23rd. With this in view one cannot but wonder if the Fallowfield line could not have formed part of the Metrolink system too. Indeed, the spacious and well-equipped depot at Reddish had been earmarked for use as an "LRT" depot and staff were retained after closure for that purpose for close on two years. The section east from Levenshulme had been re-laid latterly with concrete-sleepered track and the OHL was still in place from Fairfield Junction. But ever is hindsight 20/20 vision!

*The author would like to finish this section by offering a few words to honour the memory of Mr.A.W. (Bill) Wood who died in 2008. Bill was both a gentleman and a scholar whose memories of his years as a signalman at Chorlton Junction and elsewhere enhanced my knowledge of this ever-fascinating railway.*

**Between Audenshaw Junction and Fairfield, c.mid-1930s:** Looking west towards Fairfield Junction. Take a good look at the group of eight men posing for Mr.Lees' camera. Permanent way staff – often known as "Gangers", "Lengthmen" or "Platelayers" – or maybe these chaps were linesmen engaged in signalling operations . Alas, these men have received scant attention from railway writers over the years. Yet without the dedication of such people the railway could not have operated. Always working outside, in all weathers, and under hazardous conditions, their lot, like Gilbert & Sullivan's Policeman, was not a happy one. It has become almost a cliché in railway writing to use words to the effect: "...and not a hi-viz vest in sight." Yet it must be stated that in 1934 there were 20 fatalities on Britain's railways to personnel, eight involving permanent way workers. Mr.Bound's signals are clearly visible: the higher ones, pegged "off" are the Down Starters for Audenshaw Junction whilst beneath are the Distants for Fairfield Junction; the arm offset to the left is for the Fallowfield line. Seen on the left is the "fog hut" and two levers for detonator placers, one each for fast and slow lines; a necessary contingency in foggy weather. Spanning the tracks in the background is Lumb Lane; listed in the LNER structures register as bridge No.23, this is the thoroughfare that connects Audenshaw Road with Manchester Road. *William Lees*

## AUDENSHAW AND THE LOST JUNCTION

Moving away from Fairfield in the direction of Guide Bridge the railway continues through the township of Audenshaw. Historically the area was a mixture of farms interspersed with a substantial variety of industries: brick-making, coal mining, leather production, a linoleum factory, factories for hat-making, fur and rubber goods, the world-renowned Jones sewing machines and a wadding factory. At the western side of the township was established Messrs.Robertson's, the well-known marmalade and jam works, although we musn't mention their politically-incorrect trademark! The landscape on the railway's south side had been altered drastically in 1884 when the three Audenshaw reservoirs were commissioned. These held some 1.4 million gallons of water piped down from the Longdendale Valley (fringed by the Woodhead line) to supply the needs of Manchester. Two of the reservoirs survive today (though not in use for water supply) alongside the M60 motorway which occasionally floods due to seepage. Some three-quarters of a mile east of Fairfield Junction was sited Audenshaw's "lost junction". Part of the Oldham, Ashton & Guide Bridge Railway (OA&GB), this was Audenshaw Junction West where a curve, 28 chains long, veered north to join the connecting line running north from the GC main line at Stockport Junction. The joining point was known as "Canal Junction" due to its proximity to the Ashton Canal. The OA&GB line then proceeded via Crowthorn Junction (where the line from Denton Junction joined) and along via Ashton Moss South and North junctions to join the L&Y's main line ("The Ashton Branch") from Manchester Victoria to Stalybridge. A short distance along the L&Y main line a second section of the OA&GB, three miles long, reached Oldham (Clegg Street). A joint concern managed by the GCR and the LNW, the OA&GB was incorporated in 1857 and survived as an independent entity until Nationalisation. The connecting curve from Audenshaw Junction West was taken out of use in June 1938. Little seems to be known as to what traffic used it, although an MS&L timetable dated April 1877 shows a service from Liverpool to Oldham which travelled this way to avoid Guide Bridge. After closure of the Guide Bridge avoiding line the crossovers from fast to slow lines and vice-versa, part of the original junction layout, were retained and kept the "Audenshaw Junction" title, though now under the control of the signalbox at Stockport Junction. Late in the evening of 20th May 1970 an EMU travelling from Manchester to Hadfield was derailed here; the unit overturning and causing two fatalities. Though mystifying the authorities at first, the accident was later pinpointed to malpractices in Stockport Junction box where a signalman had been in the habit of short-circuiting the electric locking mechanism on the lever slides to speed up operations, thus allowing points to be moved earlier than they otherwise could be. The "new" junction and the quadrupled track all disappeared in the 1973 rationalisation. Sadly, Audenshaw Junction will not be remembered for its connections, or for the splendid array of signals, but for a needless and entirely avoidable accident.

**Lumb Lane Crossing c.1900:** Prior to the widening between Fairfield and Guide Bridge Lumb Lane, then just a cart track, crossed the railway on the flat via a simple crossing – a common feature all over the railway system in the days when traffic, both road and rail, was less intense. A group of boys gaze at the photographer in this picture looking north towards the Ashton Canal and Manchester Road. The rural flavour embodied here is captured beautifully by Frank Pritchard in his book: "East Manchester Remembered". Even in the 1920s and '30s the area still possessed something of a bucolic charm. Frank writes: *"Many people from Openshaw, Gorton and Longsight districts caught the No.19 single-decker bus to Droylsden Station, Lumb Lane. Then they had a pleasant stroll along the lane, through the hamlet of Littlemoss to Newmarket Road and turned left to pass over the (Ashton) canal. A quarter of a mile further on was Daisy Nook, where they would join the merry crowd to enjoy all the fun of the fair."* Notice the signals to the right of the crossing-keeper's house: the splitting home arms for Audenshaw Junction just ahead. Dow records that crosing keepers were paid 18/- a week (90p) in the railway's early years.

*Tameside MBC Archives collection*

**Page 76 (over page)**

**Audenshaw Junction, c.mid-1930s:** Pictures taken at Audenshaw Junction until recent years numbered just one. So it was with delight that I stumbled a few years ago across a series of glass plates, believed to have been taken by the Manchester press photographer, William Lees. "Bill" Lees worked for the old Kemsley newspaper group in Withy Grove, Manchester and, apart from being an obviously competent photographer, was an ardent railway enthusiast to boot. Little of his work has come to light previously, so Woodhead enthusiasts can indulge themselves with this splendid shot of B7 class No.5470 storming along the Up Fast line with a special (No.466) bound, in all probability for one of the East Coast resorts – typically Cleethorpes, Skegness or Great Yarmouth. In contrast to the make-up of similar contemporary workings, the train is comprised of Gresley corridor stock. Before you admire Mr.Bound's splendid signals, spare a thought for the lamp men who had to perform trapeze-like manoeuvres up those spindly ladders in all weathers to replenish the oil lamps for the top home and distant arms. The semaphore arms are air-operated, the cylinders can be seen below the arms. Electro-pneumatic operation had not long come into operation. Branching left, about a hundred yards ahead of the loco is the aforementioned OA&GB connecting line avoiding Guide Bridge and re-joining the Stalybridge Branch at Canal Junction.

*William Lees*

**Between Audenshaw Junction & Guide Bridge, c.1947**: Moving away from Audenshaw towards Guide Bridge the GCR main line was fringed by a cosmopolitan landscape comprising post-WWI housing, recreation grounds and industry. Heading towards Manchester C13 No.E7410 hauling a local train passes the Lumb Lane recreation ground. In the background can be seen the pitheads of the New Moss Colliery in Ashton-under-Lyne, while striding past on a shallow embankment is the previously-mentioned "Snipe" line of the former LNWR coming up from Ashton Moss Junction. Today's Snipe retail park covers the land here today.

*H.S.T.Parrish*

**Audenshaw, c.1951:** K3 No.61960 runs down towards Fairfield with the Down Harwich boat train, aka *The North Country Continental.* The view looks from the Audenshaw Road overbridge (B6390) and towards Lumb Lane close to where we saw the gangers and the level crossing in the previous pictures. The train, a mixture of eleven different coaches, is almost worthy of a study in itself. In the distance, beyond the neat inter-war semi-detached houses of Audenshaw, stand the mill buildings so typical of the Guide Bridge area – all dominated by the Pennine fringe seen faintly in the far background.

*Geoff Parrish*

**Western approach to Guide Bridge, early 1950s:** Pulling away from the station with a Down express is B1 No.61268. In the background a light engine makes its way into the station, marked by the faint outlines of St.Stephen's church, always a landmark here. Stockport Junction branches away to the right; the line along from here to Crowthorn Junction goes off to the left.

*Raymond McCarthy*

## GUIDE BRIDGE (CHANGE FOR GLOSSOP & ASHTON, STALYBRIDGE & DROYLSDEN)

Known until 1845 as "Ashton & Hooley Hill", quickly shortened to plain "Ashton", the question has been raised more than once: "where is Guide Bridge?" As the original name implied, the place is actually a district of Ashton-under-Lyne, a large Lancashire town sitting in today's district of Tameside and rubbing shoulders with Stalybridge, part of which is in Cheshire. Our sub-heading once appeared on the platform nameboard; if all this sounds confusing, well, it is!

Coming to the railway, things become even more complicated. Though today the track layout at Guide Bridge has been rationalised substantially, a process begun nearly seventy years ago, the station and its immediate area have a rich legacy of railways: junctions, signalboxes, sidings and avoiding lines – all serving and tied up with a traffic pattern that, at one time, must have been of almost nightmare proportions.

In the beginning were the industries: principally cotton spinning, engineering and coal mining, with a sprinkling of minor ones – hat-making, sewing machine manufacture and rope-making thrown in. As in many other historic industrial centres the canals provided the first form of reliable bulk transport. First of these was the Ashton canal, followed by the Huddersfield Narrow and the Peak Forest. The railway arrived on the scene in 1841 as the Sheffield, Ashton-under-Lyne & Manchester, MS&L from 1846 and GCR from 1897. Originally connecting Manchester with Godley, the line opened through to Sheffield in 1845. Slowly, the area increased in complexity principally with the formation of the OA&GB lines (1857), the Ashton & Stalybridge branch with the adjacent Brookside sidings, the LNWR's Heaton Norris & Guide Bridge line (1849), the Denton & Crowthorn line serving extensive sidings at New Moss colliery (1876) and the Ashton Branch Junction ("Snipe") line. Further additions by the LNWR came in 1882 with the opening of the Denton & Dukinfield line; with connections to Stalybridge this ran south of Guide Bridge with a station at Hooley Hill. Finally, in the twentieth century, an eastern curve connecting the GC main line with the Stalybridge was opened in 1905. This was topped in 1911 by a westerly curve off the OA&GB at Ashton Moss South to join the L&Y Ashton Branch along with a set of interchange sidings, the joint property of the GC and the L&Y. All-in-all an area of some complexity.

Stockport Junction was where the GCR's main line from Manchester was joined a) by the LNWR's line (via Denton Junction) from Heaton Norris, Stockport and b) by the O&GB's line (via Crowthorn Junction) from Oldham Clegg Street and Ashton Moss junctions. Unsurprisingly, it was a busy place. A traffic census taken in July 1900 recorded 252 up and 265 down trains passing over the junction in 24 hours. No wonder the GCR wanted to quadruple the line! On the main line Stockport Junction worked to Fairfield Junction in the west and Ashton Junction, at the east end of Guide Bridge station. Along the Heaton Norris line the box worked to Cock Lane sidings, and along the OA&GB line to Crowthorn Junction. To aid passage of traffic permissive block working (for freight trains only) was authorised on the down fast line between Ashton Junction and Stockport Junction (the boxes were just 359 yards apart). Wrong line working was allowed on all four roads through the station. Bill Wood, a former signalman at Stockport Junction, recalled that if the man at that box and his counterpart at Ashton Junction were not on good terms, then life could be very difficult indeed!

**Guide Bridge, Stockport Junction, September 15th 1945:** Trains entering Guide Bridge from the west first encountered the confluence of lines that was Stockport Junction, so-named after the connection made in 1849 when the LNWR opened their line from Heaton Norris, Stockport, to this point. The junction acquired further complexity when the section of line connecting with the OA&GB railway opened in 1861. Further development of the track layout came about with the quadrupling from Gorton station to Guide Bridge in November 1906. In this view from the immediate post-war period B7 No.5481 runs into the station on the Up fast line. The line to Heaton Norris curves away to the left passing the LNW's Cock Lane sidings, while the tracks to the OA&GB system can be seen sweeping away to the right immediately behind the tender. Notice the dwarf semaphores – a pattern unique to this junction and required in this position for sighting purposes.

*H.C.Casserley*

**Guide Bridge, Stockport Junction, early 1950s:** V2 No.60870 crosses the Stockport line and heads towards Manchester with a train of empty coaching stock. Of prime interest here is the first coach, a GN & NE Joint Stock Diagram 4 matchboarded corridor third with gangways. Carrying the number E52057E it was built by the NER at York and entered traffic on April 18th 1906 as No.7. The vehicle was transferred to the GC section as No.52057 in March 1934. No withdrawal records are available, but the coach was recorded at Skegness in 1954 and carried a shopping proposal date of 1955.

*Raymond McCarthy*

## GUIDE BRIDGE - THE STATION & ASHTON JUNCTION

Guide Bridge station had been substantially rebuilt in the early years of the last century, a process begun in 1903 when the GCR's main line was quadrupled between Ardwick and Hyde Junction. Four through platforms were available to passengers. On the station's north side, alongside platforms1&2 were the up and down slow lines; on the south side platforms 3&4 carried the up and down fast lines. Platforms 2 and 3 were formed either side of an island, at the east of which was a short neck referred to as an "up spur". Guide Bridge was still a busy centre in the mid-1950s: the winter 1957/58 station departure sheet lists 169 trains scheduled to leave within the period 3.47 am to 11.49 pm. The figure does not include "SX" services and only one train is listed as "MO". In this period, of course, all the Marylebone expresses called here – at least on their outward journey. A cattle dock behind platform 4 often saw movement of Irish cattle which had to be fed and watered. In the 1950s Paddy Galvin, a station inspector, saw to such duties – the railway raising a charge of 1/6d to 1/10d per beast for his services. Two main sets of sidings were situated beyond the station's east side. On the down side, to the south, were the so-called "Liverpool Sidings" a set of six roads (later enlarged to eight) paralleled by the down goods loop No.2 which could be accessed from both Guide Bridge East and Hyde Junction signalboxes further down the line.

Ashton Junction was the point where the Stalybridge Branch diverged from the GCR main line. A box of standard GCR design, a 48-lever electro-pneumatic frame controlled operations. The box worked to the already-mentioned Stockport Junction on the station's west side, to Guide Bridge North - 530 yards along the Stalybridge line and to Guide Bridge East – 585 yards along the main line towards Hyde Junction.

Immediately across from Ashton Junction, and on the north of the station either side of the Stalybridge Branch, was a substantial siding complex some half a mile long. Though shown collectively on the OS map as "Brookside Sidings" the complex was split into smaller parts as far as railway working went. At the bottom west side the sidings were referred to as "Cabinside" or "Branch sidings", though the WTT refers to them as "Ashton Junction Sidings". Shunting hereabouts was performed by the "Spot Pilot." Ahead of these, alongside the various cotton mills and warehouses, were the actual "Brookside" sidings, while ahead and again on the west side were the sidings designated as "The Park" with Guide Bridge North box controlling operations. Shunting here was done by "The Ground Frame Pilot." Across on the opposite side of the Stalybridge line the sidings were known as "Avenue Sidings". Most of the sidings in and around Guide Bridge were not provided with road access, existing purely for exchange purposes. One exception was at Brookside, off the Stalybridge branch, which had a section dedicated to serving the local community being provided with a coal yard in which the horse and cart was still a regular sight up to the early 1950s. This yard also had a general goods section from which could be seen operating some rather ancient LNER lorries. Further along the branch, at Dukinfield Junction, the siding complex re-joined the Stalybridge line. Ahead was Dukinfield Central station, a rather seedy-looking affair with wooden platforms that straggled the Peak Forest canal. Passenger services from Stockport to Guide Bridge and from there to Stalybridge ceased on May 4th 1959 with Dukinfield Central closing at the same time.

**Guide Bridge station, c.1921:** An excellent view of the "Manchester" end of the station showing to advantage the LNWR's sidings at Cock Lane off the Stockport line. Taking centre stage is class GCR Class 1 4-6-0 No.426 *City of Chester*. The loco was fitted briefly with the "Unolco" system of oil-firing (note tender oil tank) in the summer of 1921 to alleviate the prevailing coal shortages. The first two coaches of the train are MS&L 6-wheelers, although the loco carries "express lights!" Along Cock Lane sidings a good variety of private owner wagons can be seen. Amongst these are (l-r): John Welling & Sons; Robert Heath & Low Moor; Nasmyth Wilson & Co.Ltd, Patricroft; John Smith & Co. Higher Ardwick (No.116) Manchester; John Mellor & Sons, Coal & Coke Factors (No.7) Guide Bridge; The South Yorkshire Chemical Works; E.Mark & Co. (No.12) Blackburn; - all reflecting the wide area that spawned Woodhead line traffic. The building in the background has the title emblazoned along the wall: THOS. BURNETT & CO. LTD. RAILWAY WAGON WORKS." Thomas Burnett & Co. were based at Hexthorpe, Doncaster. Properly titled "Railway Wagon Builders and Repairers", the company maintained sidings here and had works also at Gascoigne Wood, Peterborough, Swinton (Mexborough), Wigan (Springs Branch) and Willesden. *P.F.Cooke*

**Guide Bridge, Stockport Junction, c.1951:** The junction from an unusual angle. Photographer Raymond McCarthy has positioned himself in the precincts of St.Stephen's church to catch this shot of a rather traffic-soiled B1 (number not known) crossing the junction with an Up 7-coach special working. Interestingly, the fifth and sixth coaches look, possibly, like a pair of articulated former LNER "Tourist" coaches still retaining their two-tone green and cream livery. *Raymond McCarthy*

**Guide Bridge station, c.1920:** Robinson Class 8B Atlantic No.265 awaits departure at the west end of the station with an express for Manchester. By this time it had become the practice for the Marylebone expresses to change engines at Leicester, a rough half-way point between London and Manchester and given the amount of coal left in the tender, this would seem to be the case here. No.265 was turned out from Gorton Foundry in July 1904, the third of five Atlantics and one of the second batch of the type built by Beyer, Peacock & Co. for the GCR. Becoming Class C4 under the LNER the Robinson Atlantics were drafted away from front line duties after the mid-1930s. Even so, they remained active until the late 1940s, a good innings for a design that was both successful and handsome. *P.F.Cooke*

## TRAFFIC PATTERNS AT GUIDE BRIDGE – 1950s

*Guide Bridge remained a very busy place until fairly recent memory. Our sample given below – the winter 1957/58 station departure sheet - lists 169 passenger trains scheduled to leave within the period 3.47 am and 11.49 pm. This was very similar to that pertaining in the steam era which had ended a mere three years earlier.* Departing or terminating at either Manchester London Road or Central stations (except where otherwise shown), these workings can be divided broadly into the following groups:

**NOTE: In the interests of brevity only weekday *departures* are given. There were of course corresponding arrivals. Steam haulage over Woodhead had, of course, finished with the completion of the full MSW scheme from September 15th 1954.**

1) The cross-country express services ("The Boat Trains") from Liverpool Central. These reached Guide Bridge over the Fallowfield line having reversed in Manchester Central. In 1957 there were trains to Hull at 10.51 am and 6.08 pm and to Harwich at 2.43 pm. All the Boat Trains ran via our "Woodhead" route and all called at Sheffield Victoria.

   b) A daily train to Lincoln at 9.19 am (via Worksop and Retford).There was also one evening train (at 6.48) to Gainsborough.

   c) Two trains daily served Grimsby and Cleethorpes (via Brigg and Barnetby) – at 10.19 am and 5.09 pm.

   d) Trains to Sheffield Victoria (only) calling at Hadfield and Penistone and departing Guide Bridge at 7.45 am,11.42 am and 10.50 pm.

2) Express trains running via Sheffield Victoria over the former GCR's 1899 London Extension. There were four daily expresses to London Marylebone – at 8.40 am and 2.21, 4.14 and 11.10 pm. The term "Express" is used advisedly as the trains took over five hours to reach the Capital. The old GC route was then still "competing" with the ex-Midland route to St.Pancras (typically 3hrs.45 mins) and the LNW route to Euston (typically 3hrs.40 mins). In addition to the Marylebone expresses there was one daily train to Leicester – at 12.49 pm.

3) Local services from Guide Bridge fell neatly into five groups:

a) The trains to Oldham (Clegg Street) via Ashton (Oldham Road) and Park Bridge – a distance of a mere 5 miles. These ran via Stockport Junction over the OA&GB system and were worked, invariably, by the "Push-Pull" sets with a C13 4-4-2 tank in charge. Services to Oldham were augmented by six trains daily direct from Stockport (Edgeley), though these by-passed Guide Bridge using the direct line from Denton Junction via Ashton Moss Junction to Crowthorn Junction (see map).

b) Services to Stalybridge (even shorter at 2½ miles) calling at Dukinfield (Central) and Ashton (Park Parade). Reduced by 1957 to a mere six weekday trains, these, too, used a "Push-Pull" set. A second service from Stockport (Edgeley) also linked Guide Bridge with Stalybridge. Trains came off the Heaton Norris & Guide Bridge line at Stockport Junction, called at Guide Bridge and then travelled along the Stalybridge Branch to call at Dukinfield (Central) and Ashton (Park Parade). Perusal of the Guide Bridge Winter 1957 station departure sheet shows connections at Stalybridge for Huddersfield, Halifax, Dewsbury, Leeds, York, Newcastle and Hull. This, of course, was long before these places were served by trains travelling from Manchester Piccadilly, something only made possible by the Windsor Link of 1988 by-passing Manchester Victoria.

c) Trains to and from Glossop and Hadfield starting from Manchester London Road. This was a good and well-patronised service consisting of trains at half-hourly intervals from 5.29 in the morning until 11.29 at night. Within living memory the service was then (1957) in what might be termed its "third phase". Up to around 1942 trains to Glossop and Hadfield consisted of 6-wheeled stock hauled by ex-GCR 2-4-2 tank engines; after that the C13s took over and worked the service on a "Push-Pull" basis as well as with non-corridor stock. Finally, from 1954 the 3-car 1,500V dc EMUs came onstream with the stated half-hourly frequency.

d) Trains to Macclesfield (Central) and Hayfield with connections at Romiley for Marple, Strines and New Mills. (DMUs were introduced to this service from June 1957 having taken over from the A5 4-6-2 tanks).

e) Trains to Manchester (Central) via Fairfield, Fallowfield and Chorlton-cum-Hardy. As with the Stalybridge "Push-Pull" trains, this was another service on its last legs having been reduced to three trains each weekday by 1957. As mentioned previously, the service folded completely the following July.

**Guide Bridge, n.d:** A Robinson "Glenalmond" 4-6-0, thought to be No.439 *Sutton Nelthorpe,* runs into the station with a Down partially-fitted freight. Goods traffic, especially coal, was the lifeblood of the Woodhead line, so it was with particular pleasure that this pre-Grouping shot was discovered. The "Glenalmonds", or class 1A, were a small-wheeled version (5ft.4in.) of the more or less contemporary *Sir Sam Fay* express engines; as such they especially suited to freight work. Mixed Down freight trains over Woodhead, if they did not join the CLC main line at Godley Junction, were sorted for onward dispatch at several locations: at Dewsnap sidings, here at Guide Bridge, at Ashton Moss – where the GC and L&Y had interchange sidings – or at Ardwick, the latter being the GC's main depot for Manchester coal traffic. "Block" trains, for example those containing perishables: grain, meat, fish or fruit would likely as not be forwarded straight to Manchester to be dealt with at Ducie Street adjacent to London Road. *Manchester Loco Society collection*

## FREIGHT SERVICES THROUGH GUIDE BRIDGE IN 1957

The popular conception of rail-borne freight traffic in Britain is one of a gradual eclipse following the Second War when road haulage was in the ascendancy. But in the period under consideration (1957) such argument holds little water: receipts from freight, parcels and mail that year totalled £353M – around 2½ times that from passengers and over 50% up on figures from 1945. In terms of freight tonnage carried in 1957, 274 million tons were carted around the country, of which no less than 167 million tons consisted of coal and coke traffic and Woodhead, of course, was a vital artery for such movements. These totals had remained largely static since Nationalisation, though there were modest increases in the early 1950s.

So what would a contemporary observer at Guide Bridge make of the scene there if his time machine touched down just over half a century back? Though, as we have seen, the station platforms were kept busy with passenger trains, the sheer volume - and accompanying noise – of the freight traffic would be almost overwhelming – there were some 200 timetabled movements in and around the various yards in a typical weekday and that figure does not include items such as light engine movements, short "pilot ", "trip" or empty coaching stock work.

The local nerve centres were the yards at neighbouring Dewsnap, Cock Lane and Ashton Moss. A little further afield was Mottram, with Godley Junction and Brookfold sidings centred in between. It was at Godley Junction that steam still held sway for onward traffic to Merseyside; the requisite traction change-over proving to be the Achilles Heel in the much-vaunted MSW scheme – the so-called "Britain's New Railway." And though one of the LNER's objectives in building Mottram yard back in 1935 had been to alleviate pressure on the sidings at Guide Bridge, there was still more than enough traffic to keep the place busy all those years afterwards.

Freight traffic at Guide Bridge in 1957 covered a broad spectrum. Coal was still a major player as the nation's fuel – as recently as 1963 some 60% of the coal supplied to the nation's power stations was transported by rail. Coal traffic, of course, had been the very reason for the Woodhead electrification and the sight of the Bo+Bos with their clattering and rumbling retinue of loose-coupled coal wagons were a familiar sight at Guide Bridge, Dewsnap and Ashton Moss.

Coal aside, there was still a deal of engineering industry in North-West England half a century back. All this manufacturing that demanded the "black diamonds" as well as oil for fuel, with steel, iron, clay, chemicals and timber for associated operations. The various Clean Air Acts, North Sea oil and gas were yet to rear up. Back at Guide Bridge all this work revolved round the clock of course. The first recorded movement to Ardwick Yard moved out of the Park sidings at 12.01am.

**Guide Bridge, September 19th 1933:** 04 No.6306 (one of the ROD NB Loco batch of 1918) has crossed Guide Bridge East Junction and is approaching the station complex with the 7.28 am Coal train from Worksop to Guide Bridge yard. A working timetable of the period shows such a train – comprised of around 40 wagons - allowed some four hours for the journey. Totally unremarkable, yet entirely typical of traffic over Woodhead at that time. In the background Astley Street bridge, Dukinfield, spans the tracks with Guide Bridge East Junction signalbox faintly visible at the rear end of the train.

*R.D.Pollard/Manchester Loco Society*

**Freight traffic at Guide Bridge is summarised thus:**

## DOWN DIRECTION

a) Traffic that had been received, shunted and sorted for onward dispatch from the Park, the Avenue, Ashton Junction and the Liverpool sidings. Typically trains were onward bound from these points for Ardwick Yard, Ashburys, Ashton Moss (the joint GC&LY exchange sidings just off the OA&GB line). A former signalman from Stockport Junction recalled with some mirth how one of the Pilot engines (No.9 in the WTT) had often to be hastily summoned to give "The Mossers" a shove in the back end up towards Crowthorn Junction – even an A4 was once reputedly pressed into service! Round the corner were Cock Lane sidings (ex-LNWR) and another point of despatch. The list continues to include workings to Ellesmere Port, Fairfield, Garston (Liverpool), Heaton Norris (Stockport), Lowton St.Mary's (close to Wigan and in an area then still heavily involved in coal mining). Manchester Central (Goods), Stockport (Jubilee sidings at Ash Bridge - Heaton Norris), Trafford Park, Walton and Brunswick (both Liverpool) and Widnes (site of a huge complex belonging to the chemical industry).

b) Through long-distance freight traffic not calling or requiring to be shunted: Principally, these were: Barnsley Junction to Brunswick, Broughton Lane to Ellesmere Port, Dringhouses (York) to Walton, Whitemoor and Colwick to Manchester (Ducie Street and Ardwick).

c) Freight of a local or semi-local nature: Much of this emanated from Mottram Yard (which will be covered later on) and neighbouring Dewsnap sidings. Destinations from Mottram and Dewsnap included: Ardwick, Ashburys, Ashton Moss, Brunswick, Cornbrook, Glazebrook, Manchester (Ducie Street), Northwich (Chemicals and Salt), Ordsall Lane (Salford), Shotwick (near Ellesmere Port) and Trafford Park.

Other workings: Stalybridge (LMR) to Jubilee Sidings (Heaton Norris), "Cripples" – Dewsnap Sidings to Gorton works (for repairs) and Ashton Junction to Denton (LMR). The passage of light engines is worth recording; these included: Heaton Mersey-Newton Heath, Darnall-Gorton (batches of steam locos for repair hauled "dead" by electric traction), Mexborough-Gorton (do.), Edgeley-Godley Junction, Gorton-Guide Bridge, Gorton-Gowhole (the freight transfer yard near New Mills) and Denton-Guide Bridge.

## UP DIRECTION

For reasons of geography and traffic freight patterns on the up side were not a mirror image of the down workings.

a) Traffic arriving into the various local sidings pending sorting for onward despatch over the up lines: Adswood (LMR on the Stockport-Crewe line), Arpley, Bescot, Birkenhead, Brunswick (for Dewsnap), Crewe, Glazebrook, Mansfield, Mold Junction, Stanlow (oil refinery), Trafford Park.

b) Through traffic not timetabled to call at Guide Bridge: Ardwick East-Grimsby (Fish Empties), Hull, King's Cross, New England & Woodford, Ashburys-Wath, Whitemoor & Dewsnap, Ashton Moss-Heaton Mersey, Birkenhead-Neville Hill (Leeds), Birkenhead-York (Cattle), Birkenhead-Copley Hill (SW of Leeds), Birkenhead-Hexthorpe, Copley Hill-Macclesfield (via Guide Bridge East), Denton-Warsop, Glazebrook-Darfield Main, Glazebrook-Warsop & Wath, Hillhouses-Camden (via Guide Bridge East), Huskisson (Liverpool)-Dewsnap & Dringhouses, Stretford-Woolley Colliery (Barnsley), Trafford Park-Colwick,Wharncliffe Woodmoor & York, Walton- Dewsnap, Ickles (Masborough) & York, Wigan-Dewsnap.

## SHUNTING & PILOT DUTIES

Such a complex web of movements required a great deal of work from the shunting engines. In the 1950s there were no less than eleven "Pilot" and "Trip" turns working the various yards at Guide Bridge and Dewsnap sidings and trotting out to Mottram, Newton, Fallowfield, Hyde Junction and Stalybridge. All were worked by Gorton men on a three-shift basis - centred on Guide Bridge (including Dewsnap sidings). An office on platform 1 served as a signing-on point, the place being the charge of Frank Rushton. Frank's official designation was "Telephone Attendant", though he had to issue the usual notices, along with oil and sponge cloths, etc. The word "Pilot" was well embedded into the local railway vernacular hereabouts and covered a whole host of sundry freight duties. Historically, N4 and N5 0-6-2 tank engines had been used – something dating well back into GC days. More common in the 1950s were the J11 0-6-0s – the GC's seemingly immortal "Pom-Poms" - with J94 saddle tanks helping out and assisted by locos overhauled at Gorton and needing running-in. This brought Q1 0-8-0 tanks, L1 2-6-4 tanks and even the "Wath Daisies" – the Robinson S1 0-8-4 tanks to Pilot duty. After 1958 when LMR ownership encroached, "Crab" 2-6-0s became quite common.

The longest slog was endured by No.1 Pilot which was on duty at Dewsnap from 12.45 am on Mondays to 6.00 am Sundays. Others arrived from Gorton between 4.30 and 9.30 am working through the week until between 6.00 and 11.30 pm on Saturdays. Even the C13 "Push-Pull" locos were press-ganged into working short "Pilot" trips to Ashton (Park Parade) and Fairfield. More diverse Pilot duties included shunting the sidings of Messrs.Robinson and Kershaw (the company produced armoured vehicles in part of the former GC's carriage and wagon works at Dukinfield) as well as clearing repaired wagons; Dukinfield having been inundated with repair work in the wake of WWII. One Pilot turn was nicknamed "The Marigold" after the popular flower of the time. But why this fascinating name should have been bestowed on a J11 whose duties consisted of trotting back and forth from Guide Bridge to Dewsnap sidings with a few wagons remains something of a mystery.

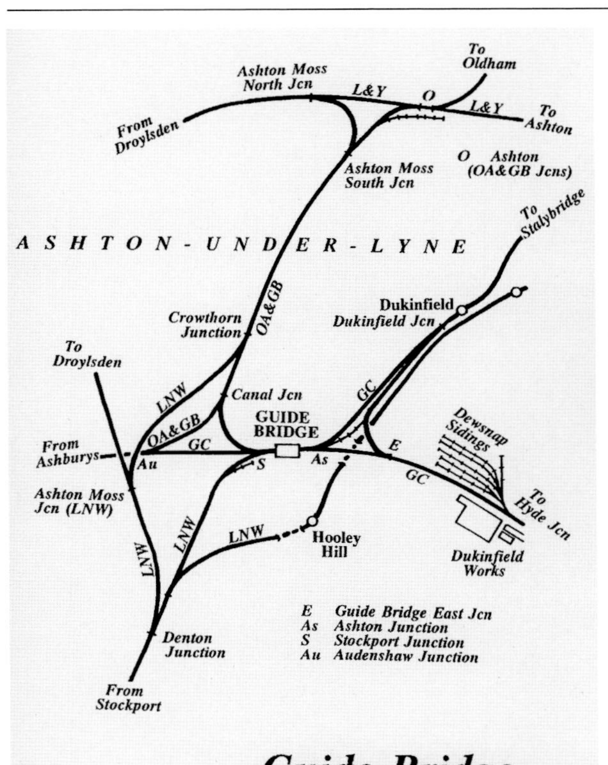

**Guide Bridge, c.1951:** Getting the "peg" at the east end of platform 1 is "Director" - by now Class D11/1 - No.62665 *Mons* is on a rather unusual working. By then allocated to Heaton Mersey (9F) the loco is seen working a Halewood-Dewsnap goods. *Mons* had already worked the Down Mail train from Marylebone to Liverpool from Godley Junction.

*Geoff Parrish*

**Guide Bridge station, c.1920:** Seen alongside platform 3 is 9P No.1167 *Lloyd George* at the head of an express for Marylebone. Made up to, typically, around nine coaches, the first vehicle is one of the 60ft."Matchboard" vehicles built at Dukinfield from 1911. However, despite the size and power of the latest Robinson creations, it is recorded that some Gorton drivers maintained a preference for their "Directors" on the London trains. Thus the 4-4-0s remained on the fastest Marylebone expresses, with the 9Ps working principally the slower 3.50pm Up from London Road and the 8.45 am Down. *Lloyd George* lost his name in 1923, removed, it is said, on the orders of Sir Frederick Banbury. The plates were not discovered until 1963 when King's Cross loco - "Top Shed" was under demolition.

*P.F.Cooke*

**Guide Bridge station, c.1921:** A low evening sun highlights this scene depicting part of the station rarely photographed. The view looks across the running lines on the station's east side. The background is dominated by the premises of Messrs.Scott & Hodgson Ltd. – a company who were notable engineers and were established here in 1854. Aside from being producers of boilers and mill engines up to 3000 hp, Scott & Hodgson were ironfounders, millwrights and gear manufacturers, employing up to 350 people around the time of the First War. A former railwayman based at Guide Bridge recalled seeing a team of eight horses pulling the company's road wagons along Guide Lane and over the bridge to Ashton and Audenshaw. In front of the works a Class 8A "Kitson Tiny" 0-8-0 No.1134 waits between duties; while off to the right, Class 1 4-6-0 No.423 *Sir Sam Fay* has reversed to collect a horse box from the dock adjacent to platform 4. *Sir Sam*, is fitted with "Unolco" oil-burning gear, a contingency applied in the summer of 1921. A small memento of the Scott & Hodgson factory survives today as Scott Gate, a thoroughfare on the latter-day housing estate that covers part of Cock Lane sidings off Guide Lane on the station's south face.

*P.F.Cooke*

**Guide Bridge, eastern approaches, May 1951:** One of the finest steam era pictures ever taken here must be this one: B1 No.61182 enters the station with a Down express. Just look at the volume of traffic; the O4 waiting to come off the Stalybridge branch, the two light engines in the yard, the variety of the freight wagons dotted here, there and everywhere – and not a hint of modern traction to be seen!

*J.Davenport/B.K.B.Green*

**Guide Bridge station, c.1920/21:** P.F.Cooke was the undisputed master of the railway photographer's art in and around Manchester in the immediate pre and post-Group years. Seen waiting to leave the station in one of his finest views is an Up express with Class 8B Atlantic No.262 piloting "Director" Class 11F No.507 *Gerard Powys Dewhurst*. The sight of these two engines, both examples of Robinson's best designs, forging up the long grades towards Woodhead must have been truly breathtaking. Alas, Cooke left behind him no records of what he photographed; all we have to go on is that this is an Up express hauled, unusually for the GC, by two locomotives. Behind the train engine's tender can be seen one of the iconic "Barnum" coaches. Slab-sided and 59ft.11in.long, the vehicles were amongst the first products of the new Carriage and Wagon works at Dukinfield in 1911. No.262 was the third of the last batch of eight simple Atlantics and was completed at Gorton in March 1906. *Gerard Powys Dewhurst* (so-named after one of the GC's Directors, hence the name of the class) emerged from Gorton in February 1920. Looking closely at the loco with its mirror-like finish and spotless condition, it is possible that this is either one of No.507's first main line outings or a return to Neasden (home shed until March 1924) after its first overhaul at Gorton – November 1921. In the background, the tower of St.Stephen's church, the pneumatic semaphores, various mill chimneys and Gartside's Brookside Brewery provide the finishing touches to this superb view, something, surely, worthy of the award "Best in Class". *P.F.Cooke*

**Ashton Junction, c.1948/49:** The east end of Guide Bridge station was dominated by three key features: the lattice footbridge spanning the tracks from the station's south side over to the canal on the north; the goods warehouse and offices along the line's Up side and Ashton Junction signalbox which controlled operations through the station and along the Stalybridge branch. All three elements appear in this view of B1 No.61316 immaculate in lined BR apple green entering the station with a down express, possibly a cross-country working from Hull or Harwich. *H.S.T.Parrish*

**Guide Bridge, August 10th 1935:** J39 No.2703 pulls away from platform 1 with the 3.52 afternoon stopping train from Manchester London Road to Sheffield Victoria. Ex-LNE signalman, Ronnie Gee, recalls that such workings were referred to as "The Ord" – meaning "Ordinary Passenger". Certainly, this train – made up of nine or so mostly ex-GCR carriages – was "ordinary"; but perhaps "Extraordinary" might be a term more apt. "All stations" – well, not quite, but near enough - the 3.52 made no less than fifteen stops en route over Woodhead to Sheffield (a corresponding Down service left Sheffield at 7.10 am). The maximum time the train was moving was for the 15 minutes allowed between London Road and Guide Bridge. Clearly, the service provided as a once a day connection for all the souls living east of Hadfield with the two northern cities. Even on Sundays "The Ord" obliged, though the morning train (at 9.10) terminated at Penistone and the afternoon service (at 3.35) missed out Woodhead, Oughty Bridge and Neepsend. At 1 hour, 43 minutes a trip on the weekday "Ord" must have been just a mite tedious.

*R.D.Pollard/Manchester Loco Society*

**See page 89**……

**Page 88 (previous page)**

**Guide Bridge station, July 10th 1935:** A welcome follow-on to the picture of the 12.40 express to Cleethorpes, seen at London Road. Here, drawing away from the station with the same train, is B3 4-6-0 No.6169 *Lord Faringdon*. The first four coaches make up the Cleethorpes portion, the remaining three were for Hull – detached, again, at Sheffield. Behind the tender (looking remarkably like a GWR vehicle) is a GCR 50ft. non-corridor clerestory brake lavatory third of 1903; next is a 60ft.non-corridor, ten-compartment "Matchboard" coach, a Dukinfield product of 1911; the third vehicle is similar, but is a 60ft. lavatory composite; the fourth coach is the same pattern as the first, but is turned about-face. The three rear coaches, making up the Hull portion, are (by then) standard Gresley corridors; the first coach looks like an early pattern with doors to each compartment. *Lord Faringdon* had been allocated to Gorton after its sojourn over the GN main line. In summer 1935 it was a Gorton engine, thereafter moving east to Immingham towards the end of the year. After almost exactly two years back at Gorton (1942-44) it was dispatched south to Neasden before returning again to Immingham and finally to Lincoln from where it was withdrawn on December 6th 1947. As LNER No.1494 *Lord Faringdon* was cut up at Dukinfield. *R.D.Pollard/Manchester Loco Society*

**Guide Bridge, c.1951:** Another fine example of the use of Gresley Pacifics on the Marylebone trains. Here, well in to the post-War era, is a second example: No.60048 *Doncaster* about to leave platform 3 with an Up working. *Doncaster* was a late rebuild from A1 to A3 (1946) and still carries right-hand drive; the loco was allocated to Leicester shed when this picture was taken. Today the sight of a Pacific at Guide Bridge (and there have been quite a few in recent years) brings out the photographers in their hordes. But on this day sixty years ago only Ray McCarthy and his Leica were here to record this splendid scene for us. What looks like a train made up of Gresley corridor coaches is augmented by an ex-GCR "Barnum" behind 60048's tender. *Raymond McCarthy*

**Guide Bridge, Ashton Junction c.1951:** Pictures inside signalboxes are rare; those showing known characters even rarer. This was signalman Alec Braden, one of the "characters" working on this section of railway. Famed for his watch-repairing skills, Alec had been transferred to Ashton Junction box from Ashburys East Junction. Notice the now-familiar slides pulled out to activate the electro-pneumatic mechanism operating the various points and signals. Modernisation has yet to come to the block instruments, the box still housed the original wooden-cased variety belonging to the GCR. Alec's "cable-knit" pullover gives a period sartorial touch. *Raymond McCarthy*

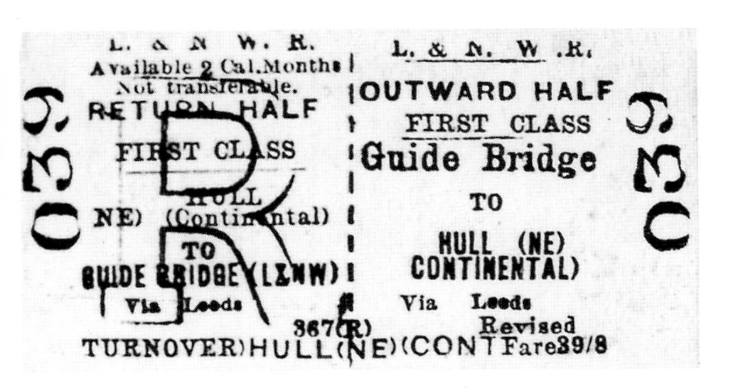

## Woodhead Diversions

Diversions away from Woodhead were commonplace, especially after the Second war when the two tunnel bores, especially that on the Up side, were in need of repair. Most commonly trains ran along the Stalybridge branch from Ashton Junction to reach the ex-L&YR main line at Stalybridge. Thence along via Diggle and the Standedge tunnels to Huddersfield. From here reversal was necessary - back to Springwood Junction and along the L&Y line crossing the splendid Lockwood viaduct to re-join the GC main line at Penistone.

*The pictures below show two such diversions along the Stalybridge branch; especially interesting as they are set in locations not often photographed.*

**Dukinfield, October 21st 1951:** B1 No.61184 enters the station with a Manchester London Road to Marylebone express. Dukinfield Junction signalbox is close by the fourth coach. From here the line led off into the north section of Brookside sidings. Just behind can be seen Spring Grove mill dating from 1818 and latterly deployed for woollen manufacture. *J.D.Darby/ Manchester Loco Society*

**Ashton Park Parade, October 21st 1951:** Today is a Sunday, a good day for diversions! B1 No.61155 (Dick Ball's engine) storms into the station with the 9.30 am Liverpool Central to Hull express. The train will have reversed in Manchester Central (due out at 10.32) before travelling over the Fallowfield line to reach Fairfield and Guide Bridge. The branch to the left is from the goods warehouse opposite Park Parade station and sited along Lower Wharf Street. *J.D.Darby/ Manchester Loco Society*

## DEWSNAP SIDINGS

Clear of Guide Bridge station, passing Ashton Junction then Guide Bridge East Junction, trains on the up line soon passed a conglomeration of sidings. Unless they caught a glimpse of the nameboard on the well set-back signalbox, few passengers would have known where they were. *Dewsnap*, what a curious name! This is an area steeped in history. The township of Dukinfield has origins going back to the 13th century. One, Colonel Robert Duckenfield was a Puritan who became commander of Cromwell's army in North-West England in 1648. The family owned Dukinfield Hall which stood on land to the north-east side of the Peak Forest Canal, all well to the south of the railway. The noble hall lasted until demolition in 1950.

Long before the arrival of the railway, cotton spinning and coal mining were well-established in the Dukinfield area. Most of the mills were sited around the River Tame, the Huddersfield Canal and close to Dukinfield station on the Stalybridge branch. As mentioned earlier, this line ran north-east from the MS&L's main line at Ashton Junction. Three coal mines – Dewsnap collery, Dewsnap New Pit and Astley's New Pit were clustered around the MS&L's main line in the Dukinfield area and both the Astley pit and the Dewsnap colliery were connected to the railway. An arm off the nearby Peak Forest canal (qv railway ownership) had previously served the Dewsnap workings. A Tithe map dated 1850 shows a branch leading into the MS&L main line. This connected with a tramway north-east of Dewsnap Lane which led up from Newton Wood via an inclined embankment.

West of the collieries, crossing the line, was a curiously-named thoroughfare - Dog Lane. A wagon repair depot had once existed here, but Dow records it closing in 1861 with work transferred to Gorton. Sidings at Dog Lane, along with a coal wharf are shown on an early MS&L map. These lay on the north-east side of the main line and it was on this site, at a later date, that the Dewsnap sidings were laid. The precise opening date of the full complex is obscure, but it must have occurred after 1901 when the Astley colliery, which took up a substantial area west of the junction with King Street and Globe Lane, closed.

The sidings consisted originally of fourteen roads, but the number was extended in the early years of the twentieth century to no less than 56, all laid parallel to the running lines. Like their counterparts at Guide Bridge, Dewsnap sidings existed for sorting and transfer work, there was no road access. Much traffic emanated from Merseyside and this continued right up into modern times. Travelling via the Fallowfield line to avoid Manchester, the two Liverpool depots of Huskisson and Brunswick supplied much traffic for Dewsnap. Railway lore gave the various roads odd names: "Dog Lane" (where the works and wagon repair were), "Klondyke", "Kelly" and "Back Slip" all resounded night and day to the sound of wagons clattering and banging. Twelve houses for inspectors were maintained by "the company" on Astley Street, close to the GCR's Dukinfield coach and wagon works. Pity the poor shunters whose misdemeanours caused wagons to smash into the stop blocks at the siding ends, disturbing the Gaffers' precious sleep in the small hours!

More GCR history could be gleaned across on the opposite side of the line where, in 1910, the GCR opened their Dukinfield carriage and wagon works on land formerly occupied by Dewsnap colliery. A "state of the art" works enabled all carriage and wagon production previously carried on at Gorton, to be transferred here. Dukinfield works was a victim of the depression in the 1930s and many men had to transfer to other LNER carriage works, notably to York. After the Second war Dukinfield works took on the melancholy task of cutting up many former GCR locomotives, notably Atlantics and many of the various 4-6-0 classes that had been displaced by the arrival of the new Thompson B1s. Slightly later, the works was chosen to fit out electric and running gear to the newly-built EM1 and EM2 electric locomotives. With Dewsnap sidings then fully wired and the works opposite busy with traction work the Dukinfield area can be described as having played a major part in the dawn of the new era that spelled out the demise of steam over Woodhead.

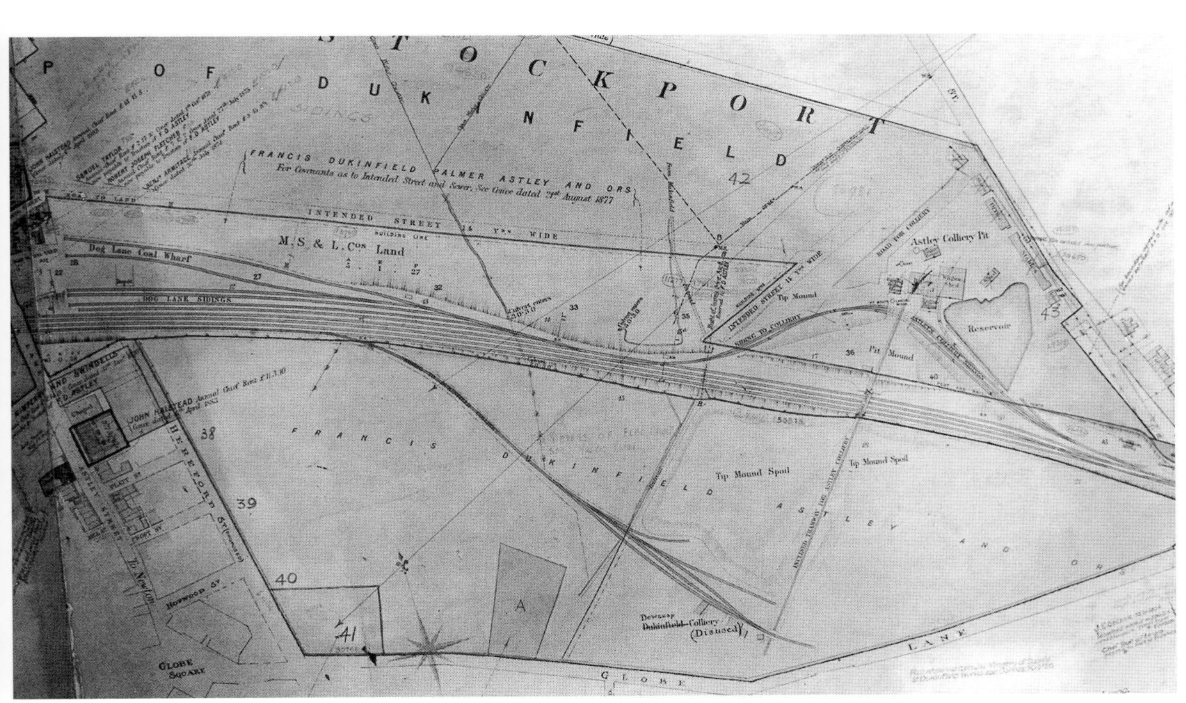


**A section from an official MS&LR line plan showing the outline of the Dewsnap area before the arrival of the siding complex and the GCR's carraiage & wagon works.**
***Collection of Frank Gradwell***

**Dukinfield, May 27th 1907:** A contemporary photograph showing the GCR's new carriage and wagon works well on the way to completion. "Craven & Markham" refers to the joint venture of Craven Brothers of Manchester and Markham & Co of Chesterfield who were awarded the building contract for the sum of £165,000. The electric sub-station or "power house" to the left was fitted out by the Brush Electrical Engineering Company at a cost of almost £20,000. Dukinfield Works opened in 1910 with J.A.Adey as works manager. The view is taken from Globe Lane and looks east.

*Collection of Terry Holtby*

**Dukinfield Works, March 13th 1948:** A melancholy sight which, perhaps sadly, was typical of the goings-on at Dukinfield in its latter days. Though steam enthusiasts may find scenes such as this one distressing, it was a fact of life that the steam engine was a mere machine that was built to perform a task. And once life-expired, then the machine was disposed of. Displaying little signs of her once regal-looking glory; shorn of most of her cab, firebox, boiler and nameplates, the mortal remains of former Class 8C Robinson Compound Atlantic (LNE Class C5) *Lady Faringdon* now numbered 2897 await the cutter's torch.

*H.C.Casserley*

**Page 93 (next page)**

**Dukinfield Carriage & Wagon Works, c.mid-1930s:** "Ayup, lad – 'e's off't roared." So, in Ashton-under-Lyne district vernacular, might the incident seen here have been described by the men around at the time. N5 0-6-2 tank No.5530 has become derailed on the pointwork leading away from alongside the carriage and wagon works. Emergency measures have been put in place by packing the loco's front buffer beam with timber baulks to prevent any further listing. Along the Down goods line – which led from Hyde Junction to Guide Bridge – the "Cavalry" in the shape of the Gorton breakdown train (and crane) drawn by B7 4-6-0 No.5476, has arrived to right the stricken locomotive. A lone observer on Astley Street glances down on the proceedings, while three railwaymen observe the photographer catch the scene on his glass quarter-plate negative. The twin-gabled building on the left was the power house at Dukinfield Works seen previously and supplying the necessary electric current and compressed air for the fabled (now) electro-pneumatically-operated points and signals along this stretch of line.

*William Lees*

**Dewsnap Sidings, c.1936:** Caprotti-fitted Class B3/2 No.6168 *Lord Stuart of Wortley* storms past the entrance to Dewsnap Sidings with an Up express; the first two coaches – elderly GC vehicles behind a van – suggesting a train for Cleethorpes. The locomotive – then allocated to Gorton – appears in its third incarnation as a poppet valve engine; notice the covers over the cam boxes above the cylinders have now been removed completely in the quest to avoid overheating. The last of the B3 sextet to be built, No.6168 was the first to go; withdrawal taking place in September 1946. *William Lees*

**Approaching Dewsnap Sidings, early 1950s:** A C14 4-4-2 tank, number unknown, passes over the Peak Forest Canal and heads east towards Hyde Junction with a local train. Opened in 1799 the canal was built to move limestone from the Dove Holes area of Buxton from a basin at Bugsworth. About half a mile after passing beneath the railway here, the Peak Forest joins the Ashton Canal at Dukinfield Junction. The waterway passed into railway ownership (to the SAuL&M) in 1846. In the years after this picture was taken, the canal fell into disuse. A vigorous campaign in the 1970s saw the canal restored and it is now an important leisure facility. *Geoff Parrish*

**Dewsnap Sidings, March 8th 1953:** B1 No.61182 brings the eight carriages of the 9.30 am Liverpool to Hull express up the rising 1-in-77/1-in-97 gradient and along towards Hyde Junction. The loco will have brought the train from Manchester Central (after reversal) along the Fallowfield line to join the main line at Fairfield Junction. Astley Street (at one time "Astley Lane" or "Dog Lane") bridge - No.30 – can be seen in the background together with the splitting signals for the northerly curve to the Stalybridge branch from Guide Bridge East Junction. Off to the right, a mixture of open wagons, typical of the period, betrays the existence of Dewsnap Sidings alive with all manner of freight transfer traffic. Alongside the Down goods line on the left is the perimeter fence of the Dukinfield Carriage & Wagon works. And though the "overhead" is prominent now, steam still has some eighteen months or so life in it yet. *BKB Green*

## ON TO HYDE JUNCTION

**Page 95 (previous page)**

**Approaching Hyde Junction, June 2nd 1934:** "Director" Class D10 4-4-0 No.5438 *Worsley Taylor* has passed under Dewsnap Bridge (structure No.30 between King Street & Victoria Road) and is heading towards the junction with the 3.50 pm Manchester London Road to Marylebone express. This, the second of the former GCR's afternoon expresses to London took a slightly different route to the 2.20 pm departure. With six vehicles behind the tender the train has made its first stop – Guide Bridge at 4.01. Next stop is Penistone at 4.40 then Sheffield Victoria at 5.02. At Woodhouse Junction the train diverged onto a section of the " Derbyshire Lines" (1892) via Chesterfield Central, due at the latter at 5.29 for a one-minute stop. After joining the more direct route via Duckmanton at Heath Junction, the 3.50 called at New Basford at 6.06, Nottingham Victoria at 6.09, Loughborough Central at 6.27, Leicester Central 6.40-6.44 and Rugby Central at 7.12. Arrival in Marylebone was due at 9.00 - a long trip! But at least passengers had the use of a restaurant car throughout the 5 hour,10 minute journey. *R.D.Pollard/Manchester Loco Society*

**Approaching Hyde Junction, April 4th 1934:** Seen from the signalbox, B17 No.2806 *Audley End* blasts its way under Wood Street overbridge and approaches the junction with the 2.05 Liverpool-Harwich express, the so-called "North Country Continental". From May 1927 this train had involved through working by both engine and men from Manchester Central to Ipswich – a distance of 216 miles. Today is the Saturday following Easter and the extra rear coaches (which look like former GC types) will have been added to cope with the extra traffic. "The Continental" will have left Liverpool Central at 2.20pm drawn, typically, by a D6 4-4-0. On arrival in Manchester Central the train will have reversed to depart at 3.22. (On weekdays the train left at 3.20). Travelling via the Fallowfield line, the main line from London Road will have been joined at Fairfield Junction. Now clear of Guide Bridge, non-stop running was the order of the day as far as Sheffield Victoria where, on weekdays, the train was divided: the rear portion going on to Cleethorpes (arriving at 7.31 pm). After a five-minute stop (4.16-4.21) the front portion got away and paid its first call at Worksop before arrival at Lincoln (5.20-5.32) where a portion from York was coupled on. The Continental now went forward to call at Ipswich at 8.31 - where engines were changed. Arrival at Harwich (Parkeston Quay) was at 9.16 and Harwich (Town) at 9.29. Passing beneath Wood Street bridge were Up and Down loops, an indication of the traffic levels here at one time: a Down loop, 1 mile, 12 chains in length stretched as far as Guide Bridge. On the Up side were two loops: No.2 - 40 chains long and No.3 (from Guide Bridge East) 51 chains in length. The spur off to the left of the Down loop is the connection leading into Dukinfield Works.

*R.D.Pollard/Manchester Loco Society*

## HYDE - A THUMBNAIL SKETCH

As with most of the surrounding districts, Hyde, a town today part of the Metropolitan conurbation of Tameside, was historically sited in Cheshire. It increased in importance with the Industrial Revolution, some forty cotton mills providing employment for the populace at one time, though their number was in decline towards the end of the nineteenth century. Hyde had a coal mine, too, though this suffered a serious setback when, in 1889 an underground explosion killed twenty-three miners.
Aside from these industries, Hyde was the home of Daniel Adamson's Newton Moor iron works. Sited just east of Hyde Junction, alongside the GCR main line, Adamson specialised in the production of mill engines and boilers. His "Manchester Boiler" with twin horizontal flue tubes became an industry standard. Using steel for his boilers Adamson dominated in this field and his products were exported all over the world. Daniel Adamson (1820-1890) was the leading promoter behind the Manchester Ship Canal. As a leading Manchester Industrialist (Adamson lived in Didsbury at "The Towers") Adamson's vision was to turn his city onto an international port. Sadly, his dream was not realised until 1894 – four years after his death.

A pivotal point in this part of the history of Manchester's railways came in March 1858 when the MS&LR opened a branch to Hyde, then a Cheshire market town. Known at first as "Hyde", the station became "Hyde Central" in 1951. The branch was later extended to Compstall and then to New Mills where, in July 1865, the Midland had arrived north from Millers Dale meeting the MS&L and laying the foundations of an enduring railway alliance – the Sheffield & Midland Joint Committee, later Great Central & Midland Joint. The station at Hyde Junction opened in February 1863; the new railway thus giving the Midland its long-cherished ambition to run trains from London (at first from King's Cross, later St.Pancras) to Manchester (London Road).
Hyde Junction was re-named Hyde North on 17th September 1951. Clearing the junction and leaving the former Sheffield & Midland Joint line curving away to the right, the rising gradient eases a little towards milepost 7 from 1-in-97 to 1-in-185. With the conurbations of east Manchester and the fringes of Ashton-under-Lyne and Stockport shaken off, the Woodhead line is now heading towards open countryside.
Though the MS&L provided no platforms for its main (Sheffield) line at Hyde Junction, the town's railway clientéle was served by the junction station's branch platforms, the Hyde (later "Central") station of 1858 and the station a mile or so east known as "Newton for Hyde".

Today, both Hyde North (the former "Junction"), Hyde Central and Newton stations remain open. They were joined in May 1985 by a third Hyde station – "Flowery Field" lying a shade over a quarter of a mile east of Hyde Junction on the north side of Hyde and close to the town's Hyde Park district.

**Hyde Junction, March 6th 1948:** B1 4-6-0 No.1183 storms up the 1-in-97 past the Junction and along towards Newton with the 3.20 pm express to Marylebone - a fine shot taken in the early years of BR. Resplendent in apple green with black and white lining, No.1183 was turned out from Vulcan Foundry in August the previous year. When the picture was taken No.1183 was allocated to Sheffield (Darnall). As BR No.61183 the loco was condemned on July 9th 1962. *J.D.Darby/Manchester Loco Society*

**Hyde Junction, 1935:** "Director", Class D11, 4-4-0 No.5508 *Prince of Wales* crosses the junction and heads towards Newton at the head of an express for Marylebone. The photograph shows well the layout at Hyde Junction: the former GC & Midland Joint line from New Mills trails in on the left to join the main line in front of Hyde Junction signalbox. In the 1950s the stationmaster here was Mr.Moffatt who was assisted by porters Harry Archer, Frank Rowe, Ted Slater and George Visor. Manning the signalbox over the years were George Mitchell, Frank Myatt, Harold Sant and signalwoman "Madge". Over to the right the sidings with the solitary wagon belonged to Daniel Adamson & Co (he of Manchester Ship Canal fame) whose engineering works were sited a short way alongside the Up line. Behind the train can be seen the ruins of the Astley Mill which was being demolished at the time. The buildings to the left of the Joint line belonged to the Victoria Cotton Mill. The firm's boiler house was rail-connected via the single siding over to the left. The sign by the door reads: "LNER - ENGINES MUST NOT PASS THIS POINT". Spanning the tracks in the rear is the overbridge (No.31) carrying Wood Street ("The Wooden Bridge" to locals), and leading to Dewsnap Lane, beyond the railway. *William Lees*

**Hyde Junction, April 18th 1951:** Daniel Adamson's engineering works show clearly in the background as Immingham's K3 No.61827 hauls the 2.40pm Dewsnap-Grimsby fish empties along the 1-in-97 towards the station. Fish traffic had been a freight staple for the Great Central, the company having developed extensive facilities at the Humberside ports of Grimsby and Immingham; fish traffic from the former having grown massively in the 1890s. In 1902 Robinson's "Fish Engines" had appeared along with a fleet of specially-constructed 15-ton bogie Fish vans. Sadly, such traffic is another example of freight movement long gone from today's railway. *R.E.Gee*

**Hyde Junction, c.1953:** Daniel Adamson's works form a backdrop to this scene as 63643 04/7 moves away from the Sheffield & Midland Joint line and heads along towards Newton with a train of wagon empties. The locomotive had its origins in pre-Group days and loose-coupled freight trains would persist over Woodhead well into the era of electric traction. Beeching would bring in MGR trains and a belief that Woodhead had a future..............

*Norman Harrop*

**Hyde North station, April 22nd 1956:** Daniel Adamson's engineering works dominate this scene, one that recalls an historic agreement between the Midland Railway and the MS&L whereby the former company's London trains first accessed Manchester via Hyde Junction and along into London Road station. "Jubilee" No.45589 *Gwalior* (20A-Holbeck) has come off the GC main line at Hyde Junction and is en route now over the former GC & Midland Joint line via Woodley, Marple, Romiley and Strines to join the Midland main line at New Mills South Junction. The train is the diverted 2.00pm (Sundays) Manchester Central to St.Pancras express. Leaving Manchester Central the train will have travelled over the Fallowfield line from Chorlton Junction to gain the GC route at Fairfield. A pilotman will be doubtless be on the footplate to cover that part of the journey from Chorlton Junction to Romiley Junction. The diversion was due to track relaying between Chorlton and Heaton Mersey. As we saw earlier, diversions such as this were a commonplace back then; single-line working, too, was frequently used; today's ubiquitous "rail replacement" buses being largely unheard of.

*Keith Thompson*

# NEWTON FOR HYDE

Newton, once a township in its own right became part of Hyde in the 1930s. Newton station is sited 2½ miles from Guide Bridge and 7¼ miles from Manchester. Opened on 1st March 1858 – in the early years of the Manchester-Sheffield railway - the station was first titled "Newton *and* Hyde", becoming "Newton *for* Hyde" exactly seven years later. At first little more than a mere shed serving a single line of railway, the later double line and extended platforms gave scope for some quite impressive buildings: fine Victorian stone-built structures with hipped and slated roofs, fretted bargeboards and stained glass windows. Set in stone on the south-facing wall of the Down platform buildings is the monogram "MSLR" still clearly visible today. On the station's west side, clear of Hyde Junction, the line passes beneath the confluence of Clarendon Road, Commercial Brow, Ashton Road & Victoria Street – Bridge No.37. Here, set back alongside the Up line were the sidings serving the Chivers jam works from where was received fruit and other produce to be processed and dispatched as the famous jams and preserves. Adjacent to the station itself was a second goods facility – a yard and large goods shed complete with an overhead travelling crane of 25-tons capacity. The latter facilitated the handling of the many boilers produced by the various manufactories in the Hyde area at one time. Coal drops, too, were provided at Newton. Sited alongside the inclined cobbled approach leading from the station, they were used regularly by the steam lorries collecting fuel for the boilers at the local ICI Rexine factory in Hyde. Moving away eastwards from Newton station with its former goods facilities the railway crosses a fine stone-built viaduct (Bridge No.39). Alas today, the roar of traffic in the vicinity is not from the Woodhead line, but from the adjacent M67 motorway.

Joe Lloyd, a doyen of the Manchester Locomotive Society and a renowned expert on loco builders Beyer, Peacock & Co., recalls his experiences at Newton station when he was a pupil at the nearby Hyde Grammar School (today's Hyde Clarendon College). *" Transferring to Hyde Grammar School (in 1941) is where I became an enthusiast and, when school closed at 4.00 pm, a few of us hurried to Newton station nearby to watch the Up Marylebone Express from London Road go through; the first "namer" I spotted was No.4474 Victor Wild. Later, I took down every loco number and not just "namers". The school building had just two classrooms with windows across the sports field to the railway line, so we looked forward to those years when glances could be taken as passing trains were heard, although this landed us in trouble with the teacher if we weren't careful standing up so we could see out. Detention was the punishment. I vividly recall an occasion when the distinctive chime whistle of an A4 was heard and practically the whole class stood up to look out – boys and girls too, much to the teacher's wrath! I cannot recall the year that occurred and the line was just too far away to read engine numbers anyway, even if one had been able to stand up long enough for a good look when the teacher's back was turned. The A4 in question was at the head of a goods train – such unusual rostering was not uncommon in those war years – and had come to a stand at the signal in advance of Hyde Junction where it was heading, the chime on the whistle being for the signalman's attention. I never did find that engine's identity."*

**Newton station, November 25th 1954:** Super power at Newton as all eyes are fixed clearly on the mighty Class U1 No.69999, the LNER's only Garratt locomotive. Although not directly a "Woodhead" locomotive, it had spent most of its existence since construction in 1925 engaged on banking coal trains up the Worsborough Incline between Wath and Silkstone West Junction. Never a popular engine and a difficult locomotive to handle, a decision was taken to convert the leviathan to oil-firing – a task completed at Gorton in 1953. Numerous test runs were made from Dewsnap Sidings to Crowden to prove the efficacy (or otherwise) of the conversion. This photograph shows the 178-ton monster engaged on one of the last trips the engine made before it left this part of the Woodhead line, though the last recorded journey hereabouts was made on February 12th 1955. In June that year, having languished at Gorton, the monster was packed off to Bromsgrove where it worked a brief spell as a Lickey Banker, though not for the first time, as the Garratt was previously deployed there from March 1949 to November 1950 when it was still a coal-burner. No.69999 was condemned in December 1955 and was cut up at Doncaster.

*B.K.B.Green*

**Newton, station approach, c.early 1950s:** Taken from below the Sheffield Road, this view shows the compact nature of the station layout in almost its entirety together with the large goods shed seen extending immediately beyond the buildings on the Down platform. Notable is the presence of the 25-ton overhead crane seen on the left and the coal drops sited on the inclined approach to the goods yard. The scene here today is unrecognisable with a multitude of light industrial buildings covering the whole area. The one-time large goods shed has been replaced by a scrap-metal processing plant forming an unsightly scar immediately behind the Down platform.
*Author's collection*

**Newton Viaduct, April 15th 1954:** Class 04/6 No.63876 has just cleared the viaduct and is en route from Ashburys to Wath Yard with a train of coal wagon empties. Perusal of working timetables shows a journey time of around 2½ hours for our train with a 10-minte stop at Crowden for water. Today is a spring day and the sun is shining. But consider a 3.20 am start from Ashburys with a similar train in the depths of winter, a freezing gale and driving snow through the Longdendale Valley followed by a suffocating 3 miles through the "hole under the hill" and the popular image that was "the glory of steam" begins to tarnish.
*B.K.B.Green*

**(Top)**

**East of Newton station, c.1953:** K2/2 No.61751 has cleared Barm House bridge (structure No.41) and appears to be making an all-out effort along the 1-in-143 towards Godley. 61751 was a Colwick engine from 1946-56 and the presence of a large number of vans suggests a returning fruit empties in the direction of East Anglia. Notice one of the loco crew is making a sharp glance in the direction of the photographer! *B.K.B.Green*

**(Right)**

**East of Newton, June 4th 1954:** Clearing Newton station and over the viaduct the Woodhead line entered a deep cutting. K3/2 No.61966 hurries along towards Godley with an Up Excursion working – 553 – to one of the East Coast resorts. Steam over Woodhead is having one of its last gasps. Today is a Friday and in ten days time electric working from Manchester as far as Penistone will commence, rendering scenes like this to the history books. *B.K.B.Green*

**Newton Goods yard, in the pre-Grouping era:** A charming photograph taken in a more leisured age when, seemingly, everyone turned out to get into the picture! The goods yard here serviced a variety of local industries in the days when Hyde and the surrounding areas were a major force in heavy engineering and the manufacture of cotton cloth. Users of Newton's facilities would have been Daniel and Joseph Adamson, Thomas Beeley, all boiler-makers, ICI (Rexine), Messrs.Ashton Bros. of Hyde, famous for towel manufacture and producers of the once-famous "Ashton's Zorbit" towels, The International Cotton Waste Company and Messrs.Newton Mill, manufacturers of stationery. On an unknown date GCR 0-6-2 tank Class 9F (LNE N5) No.536 is seen at the head of a train comprised of mostly open wagons being made ready for departure. No.536 was built by the MS&L at Gorton in 1895 and spent all of its GCR days based at the parent shed. It was withdrawn in November 1960 – a good innings of over 65 years.
*Collection of David Nixon/Manchester Loco Society*

# GODLEY JUNCTION

**To borrow a phrase from our early cinema-going days: "this is where we came in." For it was at Godley Junction where our frontispiece image – the splendid shot of B7 No.5034 coming off the CLC route – was taken.**

Godley first came to prominence in railway annals in 1841 when the Sheffield, Ashton-under-Lyne & Manchester's (SAuL&M) Manchester-Sheffield line reached these parts; Godley then being little more than a village on the Hyde to Mottram road. This first section of railway opened for business on 17th November 1841 with the first Godley station standing as a mere shack and known as "Godley Toll Bar" sited close to what is now the A57. A little over a year later the station moved east to where a junction was formed with the opening of the MS&L's branch to Apethorne Junction, north-east of Woodley, on 1st February 1866 whereupon the station became "Godley Junction". This line was transferred to the Cheshire Lines committee (CLC) ownership later that year. From a junction at Woodley itself the CLC reached Stockport (Tiviot Dale) via Brinnington Junction. West from Stockport at Skelton Junction (on the outskirts of Altrincham) the CLC expanded further in 1873 with a railway connecting at Glazebrook on the Manchester to Liverpool line. Using the Godley to Glazebrook line the MS&L had a direct line from its East Coast ports over to Liverpool and Merseyside, thus by-passing the congested lines around Manchester.

Extensive sidings were built at Godley Junction alongside the MS&L's line at the rear of the up platform and further along – ahead of the junction on the down side of the main line. The CLC had their own sidings: at Brookfold on the south side of the junction and on the line going down to Woodley Junction. Brookfold sidings possessed their own signalbox and a 70ft.loco turntable. The turntable at Godley made history when it suffered a near miss from the first bombing raid over nearby Hyde in WWII. A CLC traffic control office was sited here too and the place became a focal point during the war when one of the LNER's wartime operational headquarters opened here. Deemed to be bomb proof, the building had the luxury of parquet flooring and cast iron stoves. Controlling operations as far afield as Wath and Doncaster, it was housed in a single-storey building alongside the back of the up main line platform. At Godley Junction station a signal stores along with a smithy, fitting shed and saw mill was provided behind the up main line platform.

It was at Godley Junction that the Achilles heel of the newly electrified MSW system, dubbed "Britain's New Railway" by BR, showed itself. Here, at Brookfold Sidings, it was necessary to change traction: from steam (later diesel) to electric and vice-versa for all traffic (and there was a great deal of it) continuing its journey westbound over the CLC. A traction change-over siding was provided and two loops, one on either side of the line, ran between Godley Junction and a point some 700 yards east – "Godley East" with its own signalbox. The loops had been lengthened in the First War to enable the handling of longer coal trains. Beyond Godley East the double track formation continued through Hattersley and Broadbottom as far as Mottram No.1 signalbox.

Godley Junction station was re-named plain "Godley" in May 1974. On 7th July 1986, five years after the closure of the Woodhead line as a through route, a new station named "Godley East" opened for business sited close to the A57 road. So, some 133 years later, railway history at Godley came full circle.

**Godley Junction, May 12th 1934:** "Sams", "Sam Fays", or "Cities", GCR enginemen used all these terms to describe Robinson's Class 1 4-6-0s. We came across a "Sam" at London Road leaving with a Cleethorpes train. Here is another of the class in quite different territory. No.5424 *City of Lincoln* approaches Godley Junction station, again heading a Cleethorpes working. The first part of the train is made up from ex-GCR vehicles: "Matchboard" corridor stock – a product of Dukinfield works from 1911.To the left, below the railway, stands Station Road. Further along stand a row of cottages built here by the CLC for local railway workers. *R.D.Pollard/Manchester Loco Society*

**Godley Junction, May 12th 1934:** A picture that sums up nicely Woodhead's staple traffic, freight. An afternoon scene at Godley sees Lincoln's J39 0-6-0 No.1273 entering the station with the 3.58pm Ardwick to Lincoln freight. A contemporary working timetable shows a journey time of 6 hours 20 minutes for similar services. Six parallel siding roads ran alongside the Up line and two of these can be seen packed with vans and coal wagons; a coke wagon nestles to the rear of two DCA (*Doncaster Collieries Association*) wagons. Off to the right can be seen the signal stores behind which stood a Smiths shop, store room and saw mill. In the far background the chimney identifies the meat processing plant of Messrs.Walls, a site that brought much rail-borne traffic to Godley. Over on the left-hand side Station Road winds its way up off the main Sheffield Road (A57) before reaching the station approach.

*R.D.Pollard/Manchester Loco Society*

**Godley, early 1950s:** Darnall's K3 No.61865 dominates the scene on the Down line just west of the station. The occasion was a Sunday engineering operation – the erection of overhead masts for the forthcoming MSW electrification. Two such structures can be seen alongside the train and the operation would move steadily along: an ensemble of train-mounted auger and concrete swiftly engaged to complete the work. Along side the Up line the Walls factory reveals its presence.

*Geoff Parish*

**Godley Junction, February 28th 1953:** An enthusiast would have needed to be living on Mars not to have heard of all the recent travails and controversy surrounding A3 Pacific No.4472 *Flying Scotsman*. Now dubbed "the world's most famous steam locomotive", this celebrated steam engine has certainly had more than its fair share of publicity, both good and bad. Wind back the clock 60 years, though, and No.60103 was merely one of 78 others of its class that was hard at work over the metals of the former LNER system. Seen approaching Godley Junction station with a 9-coach Manchester to Marylebone express, *Flying Scotsman* still retains its right-hand drive and has yet to assume such later appendages as double chimney and German-style smoke deflectors. The train is about to cross bridge No.43 which carried the railway over the minor byway leading from Station Road to Godley Hill. Interestingly, when this picture was taken No.60103 had just celebrated its 30th birthday; for it was on February 24th 1923 that it entered traffic from Doncaster Works as the first new locomotive to be built by the LNER – then just as plain No.1472 and still un-named. *Neville Fields/Manchester Loco Society*

**Godley Junction, c.late 1890s:** A characterful shot in the CLC sidings showing No.161, a 2-4-0 built by the MS&L in August 1885 to the design of Charles Sacré. One of 12 Class 12A engine, it was originally numbered 541, before being re-numbered in October 1893. It was withdrawn and scrapped in May 1915.

*Collection of Joe Lloyd*

**Godley Junction station, n.d:** This was the Cheshire Lines side of Godley Junction station; where the CLC co-existed side-by-side with the GCR. The canopy over the island platform carries the buff-striped awning familiar at other CLC stations. Across on the GC's side of the station the nameboard reads: "GODLEY JUNCTION FOR GREAT CENTRAL & GREAT NORTHERN RAILWAYS AND OTHER LINES BEYOND." Notice, again, the signal shops and stores in the background, these dating from 1875. *Collection of Joe Lloyd*

**Godley Junction, CLC lines, October 1946:** Heaton Mersey's N5 0-6-2 tank No.9332 brings a train of covered wagons along the CLC line. The load may well consist of chemicals from the Runcorn or Widnes areas on Merseyside for on-going sorting and dispatch over Woodhead. Spanning the tracks in the background is Brookfold Lane; a rural-sounding name in an area which, even today, is set in a fairly pastoral landscape. *Eric Oldham*

**Godley Junction, CLC side, Friday March 23rd, 1934:** Recalling the golden era of Grand National specials is this superb shot of ex-GN 4-4-0 Class D3 No.4076 and ex-GCR 4-6-0 Class B4 No.6097 *Immingham* pulling away with a 9-coach Leeds to Aintree special – working number 11. The "Big Race" brought huge numbers of race-goers to Aintree, the majority arriving by rail over seventy years ago. The special took a complex route: from Leeds Central via Cudworth, Methley and Barnsley to join the GC main line at Penistone. From Godley Junction the train travelled over the CLC to reach Skelton Junction (near Altrincham); from here it was a more or less straight run along to Glazebrook to join the Manchester-Liverpool line. Probably the special avoided Warrington by means of the deviation line; forward to join the Southport Extension line at Halewood, then north via West Derby, over Fazakerley South and North junctions to reach the Aintree CLC station. For those readers with a leaning for The Sport of Kings "The National" that year was won by *Golden Miller* who came romping home at 8/1! *Collection of Manchester Loco Society*

**Godley Junction, CLC side, March 23rd 1936:** K3 No.1399 rests in the sidings after working a Darlington to Aintree Race special. Notice the distinctive CLC-pattern signals and the rather dilapidated station – the platform by now shorn of its canopy.
*R.D.Pollard/Manchester Loco Society*

**Godley Junction, CLC side March 29th 1935:** LNER Class C1 Atlantic No.3276 pulls away from Godley Junction with the 8.55 am express from Hull Paragon to Liverpool Central. The train called at Goole (9.28), Doncaster (9.53), Mexborough (10.10), Rotherham & Masboro' (10.21), Sheffield Victoria (10.33). Arrival at Godley was at 11.30 where a portion for Manchester (London Road) was detached. Travelling from Godley via Apethorne and Woodley Junctions, the 8.55 branched off at the latter point towards Stockport (Tiviot Dale) where a call was paid at 11.40. Skirting South Manchester the express travelled through what was then still countryside; via Cheadle and Northenden and on over one of the hubs of the CLC – Skelton Junction – then on via Partington to Glazebrook East Junction to join the CLC's main line from Manchester. Calling lastly at Warrington (Central) at 12.05 our Hull express arrived in the Merseyside port city at 12.30. In 1935 No.3276 was a Neepsend (Sheffield) engine and this train was worked from there as one part of a two-part diagram, returning from Liverpool at 4.05 pm back to Sheffield. (qv) Interestingly, today's timetables show an 08.56 departure from Hull with arrival in Liverpool (Lime Street) at 11.48. Though this requires a change at Manchester (Piccadilly), some Hull-Liverpool services do offer a quicker journey time in a shade over 3 hours. A final feature in our picture is the row of CLC cottages seen by the loco and mentioned elsewhere.

*R.D.Pollard/Manchester Loco Society*

**Godley Junction, CLC side, May 12th 1934:** Drawn by an ex-NER Class B15 and an ex-GC B7 (numbers not known) the 3.15 pm (SO) Huskisson to Dringhouses express meat train waits for the road over Woodhead. A heavy train, over 30 vans can be seen – the ensemble stretching as far back as Brookfold Sidings signalbox just visible in the far background.

*R.D.Pollard/ Manchester Loco Society*

**Godley Junction, pre-WWI:** Glory days of the GCR. Robinson Atlantic No.358 is seen in immaculate condition at the head of a Liverpool and Manchester to Cromer and Yarmouth express. With Godley Junction station receding in the distance the engine is making an all-out effort up the continuously rising gradient through Godley at 1-in-143 to the summit of the line through the Woodhead tunnel at 1-in-201. The 11-coach train is comprised of a mixture of clerestory and GC corridor stock. The unmistakable outlines of three MS&L 6-wheelers make up the front portion of the train *Author's collection*

**Godley Junction, May 31st 1947:** Moving closer to the station to yield a glimpse of the buildings, signalbox and sidings, but in set in a later period of time, is this view of sparkling brand-new B1 No.1167 pulling away with the 8.20 am Manchester to Doncaster train. Mr.Pollard's picture is a definite "first" for this loco: No.1167 is recorded as having left the Vulcan Foundry works just the previous day. Shining apple green and polished motion – truly a sight to behold. But doubtless the murk of the Woodhead tunnel will leave its marks behind.

*R.D.Pollard/ Manchester Loco Society*

**Approaching Godley Junction, May 15th 1948:** The solid and powerful-looking bulk of B7 No.1385 stands out as it slows for Godley Junction with a Spink Hill (nr.Chesterfield) to Huskisson (Liverpool) train of hopper wagons. Mottram Old Road viaduct (or "Hattersley Viaduct") and Godley East signalbox are faintly visible in the background. *R.D.Pollard/ Manchester Loco Society*

**Godley East, c.1899/1900:** A splendid period scene showing Class 11A 4-4-0 No.855 heading towards Godley Junction with a Marylebone-Manchester express. The bucolic surroundings stand ill at ease with today's scenario: Godley Junction, now long gone; the GCR main line finishing now at Hadfield and the area around Hattersley – slightly beyond – the site of a large overspill estate built by Manchester City Council in the 1960s. With coaches appearing in the early GCR livery of French Grey with chocolate lower panels, the ensemble epitomises period trains over "The New Line". Indeed, four out of the train's five vehicles are to purpose-built designs for the London Extension. The 11A locos were a Pollitt design appearing between 1897-99 specifically for working expresses over the embryonic main line. Rapidly eclipsed by Robinson's 11B 4-4-0 and then his Atlantics, the 11A (LNE D6) engines ended their days working over the CLC lines, venturing again as far as Godley Junction. No.855 was withdrawn in December 1947. *Author's collection*

## Onwards through Hattersley Cutting

Margaret Knott, a local historian recalled Hattersley thus: *"A green and pleasant oasis, where cattle and poultry roamed freely on farmland. It was a place where wild flowers and crops grew in meadows and fields smelled sweetly of fresh cut hay. Children and their bikes would free-wheel down the lanes".*

Leaving Godley East and the loops behind, the two Hattersley tunnels – dating from the opening of the line – were at one time encountered. The two bores, numbered 1 (west) and 2 (east) at some 300 and 900 yards respectively, had given the LNER civil engineers headaches akin to those experienced at Woodhead after WWII. The removal of the Hattersley tunnels between 1927-31 was well-covered in a previous volume ("Woodhead" Part I) and it is not the intention to repeat the material here. Suffice it to say that the tunnels' removal left behind the vast open slope of Hattersley cutting and a re-aligned bridge – the Mottram Old Road (A560) known as Hattersley Viaduct. Today, Hattersley has its own station – about a quarter of a mile east of the former junction at Godley and close to the point where the Godley loops terminated.

### Hattersley cutting: Two scenes typifying steam-hauled traffic through this spot.

**(Left)** Looking down from the Mottram Old Road overbridge (A560) it was a long way to the bottom of that cutting! On an unknown date in the immediate post-War era an "Austerity" 2-8-0 slogs its way eastwards with a train of wagon empties probably bound for Mottram Yard. A huge train – around 50 or so wagons appear behind the tender – the loco is probably barely exceeding walking pace. It was scenes such as this that put the case for electrification; but it would be the MGR trains that finally put paid to Woodhead's loose-coupled coal traffic. Godley East box can be glimpsed just ahead; notice the home signal for the Down loop is off for yet another freight train.
*Peter Ward*

**(Below)** A3 Class No.60102 *Sir Frederick Banbury* was the second Gresley Pacific to appear, emerging from the celebrated "Plant" at Doncaster in July 1922 as No.1471 of Class A1. In May 1952 60102 is seen just east of Godley East signalbox at the head of a Manchester London Road to Marylebone express. "Express" is, perhaps, a relative term as these trains took some 5¼ hours to cover the 205 mile journey, this time being some 57 minutes slower than the pre-War schedule. On completion of the MSW scheme in 1954 *Sir Frederick Banbury* and his five A3 Leicester compatriots were transferred away from the GC section and the era of Pacific power over the route was over. Sadly, in just four more years (1958) through expresses over the former GCR would cease too. *Jim Davenport/BKB Green collection*

**Spanning the site of the former tunnels was the impressive 5-span structure of Hattersley Viaduct. Listed as bridge No.46 the viaduct carried the A560 (Glossop to Stockport) road some 52 ft. above rail-level. Built originally in 1925 in the classic arched style, the viaduct was replaced to accommodate the wide cutting, the result of the opening-out of the two Hattersley tunnels. At the same time the road was diverted to the west of its original position.**

**(Top) Hattersley, August 12th 1933:** Class Q4 0-8-0 No.6075 is pictured hard at work along the Up line with a train of wagon empties. Of mixed parentage, only the second wagon in the train is identifiable, belonging to Carlton Collieries. Godley East's Down Distant signal stands guard in the foreground. Running along by the photographer is the abandoned track used for the removal of spoil from the tunnel opening works. Essentially a dead end siding some half a mile long, the track led into a set of five sidings and a short shunting neck. These were sited opposite an area known as Great Wood where the spoil was deposited. *R.D.Pollard/Manchester Loco Society*

**(Centre) Steam's last fling:**Dwarfed by the lofty viaduct, 04/8 No.63853 trundles through the cutting with an east-bound train of wagon empties, destination probably Mottram Yard. *Author's collection*

**(Left)** Looking east towards Mottram as C13 No.E7416 propels the London Road to Glossop and Hadfield push-pull set.The leading coach is an ex-GCR 12-wheeled Saloon. *Peter Ward*

**From Hattersely Viaduct, July 28th 1951:** A fine panorama is revealed in this picture as B1 No.61160 drops down the 1-in-462 gradient with the 9.27 am 5-coach Cleethorpes to Manchester express. Still visible, though surprisingly so, is the scar to the right of the Down line where the siding used for spoil removal was laid. The building to the top left is the Court House; Great Wood lies beyond the clump of trees in the centre foreground. *B.W.L.Brooksbank*

**Mottram station, n.d:** My late Publisher, Greg Fox, said that his ideal railway book would contain no pictures of trains! Looking west towards Godley, the photograph reveals the stone-built outlines of the Up platform buildings, contrasting with a rather plain waiting shelter on the Down side. The lattice footbridge stands in front of the brick-arched overbridge connecting Moss Lane and Hodge Lane with Mottram Road behind the station. Burdened with a variety of names over the years since its opening: variously "Broadbottom", "Mottram & Broadbottom, "Mottram", "Broadbottom for Mottram & Charlesworth" and again, plain "Broadbottom", the station survives, now in its third century of existence. *Author's collection*

**Mottram and Broadbottom, May 2nd 1953:** Gorton K3 No.61832 clears the station and heads towards the viaduct with an Up train of wagon empties. Readers will by now have formed the opinion that such traffic constituted much of Woodhead's traditional freight; they are right! Behind the photographer are the station's Down sidings; a similar set ran off the Up line, notice the impressive goods shed to the rear of the train. The houses below the railway stand along Market Street, bringing alive the classic piece of Estate Agents' jargon: "close to trains and all facilities!"

*J.D.Darby/ Manchester Loco Society*

**Mottram Viaduct, c.mid-1930s:** A C4 crosses the Etherow and heads west with an express. *William Lees*

## Mottram Viaduct

Construction of the Woodhead line had caused almost insuperable problems for the SAuL&M's contractors. The Woodhead tunnel aside, tunnels had to be bored also at Audenshaw, Hattersley, at Oxspring, Thurgoland and Bridgehouses (Sheffield). Newton viaduct has already been referred to, and here at Mottram, over the River Etherow, and further along, over Dinting Vale, two further substantial viaducts were required. (We will take a look at a third structure, that at Rumtickle – between Penistone and Sheffield – in our second volume).

Early literature invariably refers to Mottram Viaduct as the "Etherow Viaduct", but Mottram is the word used today and seems to have been in vogue as long as most people can remember, so "Mottram" it is. Construction of the viaduct swallowed 186,000 cubic feet of stone and 41,000 cubic feet of timber. The task was completed by the end of 1842 and trains began their passage over the works – 504 feet long and some 136 feet above the Etherow - on Christmas Eve that year. Substantial alterations have been made to both Mottram and Dinting viaducts over the 171 years of their existence and these will be covered more fully when we reach Dinting.

## OVER THE VIADUCT AND ON TO MOTTRAM YARD

The endless procession of coal and goods trains passing through Woodhead and on towards the various industrial centres in Lancashire, Cheshire and Merseyside had at some point to be sorted prior to their onward destination and subsequent unloading. After the CLC route to Merseyside was left behind at Godley Junction, the nearest point for sorting was Guide Bridge. But the two groups of sidings there – the "Liverpool" on the south side of the GC main line and the set at "Brookside" on the north-west side of the Stalybridge line, were not connected and movements involved much crossing of an already busy route.

After much casting around for a suitable unitary replacement site the LNER selected an area of land adjacent to their main line at Gamesley, between Dinting and Mottram and about 11 miles south- east of Manchester. Parliamentary approval was obtained in 1930. The contract for construction was awarded to Harold Arnold & Son of Doncaster and Mr.C.J.Brown, engineer of the LNER's Southern area supervised the works. This was a project on a massive scale: due to the unstable nature of the subsoil some 1½M cubic yards of spoil had to be removed from the area. Some was used to form an embankment for the main line which had to be re-aligned some sixty yards north of its previous position. A well, 300 feet deep, was sunk to enable watering of locomotives, with a 50,000 gallon storage facility being provided.

Opened in October 1935, the Gamesley site, ever-after known as Mottram yard - had eight reception sidings into which trains arriving from the east were fed. Two sets of ten sorting roads apiece were provided, each road had a holding capacity of 60 wagons (later increased to 62). The yard was worked on the gravity principle, the naturally falling gradient (1-in-200) eschewing the need for a "hump". The gradient increased to 1-in-80 when the reception sidings were reached. Points were operated by compressed air and a control tower at the east end of the complex, close to the Glossop Road (A626), watched over operations. At the yard's extremities two signalboxes, Mottram No.1 and No.2 , controlled traffic in and out of the yard.

Mottram's biggest single recipient of traffic was from Wath at the heart of the South Yorkshire coalfield and opened by the GCR in 1907. In 1951 Wath was still providing 11 trains per day, although coal traffic had peaked long before the Second War. Outside of the Yorkshire area, trains arrived from as far off as York, Grimsby and London.

### DESTINATIONS FROM MOTTRAM YARD (SIDING NOS.1-20 NORTH-SOUTH ORDER)

| | |
|---|---|
| 1) BESWICK STEEL/BRADFORD ROAD GAS | 2) BREWERY |
| 3) MIDDLETON JCT./CHADDERTON | 4) AGECROFT C.E.G.B. |
| 5) ORDSALL LANE | 6) WINDSOR BRIDGE |
| 7) CHESTER | 8) MOLD JUNCTION |
| 9) ELLESMERE PORT/STANLOW | 10) BIRKENHEAD |
| 11) ASHBURYS-ARDWICK EAST-BREDBURY | 12) ARDWICK WEST cont... |
| 13) PARTINGTON C.E.G.B | 14) TRAFFORD PARK |
| 15) ARDWICK KOBO | 16) ARDWICK DROPS |
| 17) ARPLEY/WALTON OLD JCT. | 18) WIDNES/EDGE HILL |
| 19) DEWSNAP | 20) STALEY & MILLBROOK |

At the yard's west end three further sidings, each of 20-wagon capacity, were provided for the holding of "cripples".

The run-down of Mottram yard began towards the end of steam in 1967; locomotive use aside, the deployment of coal as an industrial and domestic fuel was then in decline. In the MGR era the yard became the place for change-over from diesel to electric traction. The departure sidings were abolished and the arrival sidings were turned into six roads, each holding 85 wagons, plus an engine release road on the north side and a single shunting neck. These fed into a single departure line, re-joining the main line towards Godley Junction west of Mottram No.1 signalbox Despite the closure of the Woodhead line as a through route from 1982, the small halt used by staff working in the yard still appeared in the working timetables as late as the mid-1990s!

Consideration for the construction of the yard must have been undertaken in the mid to late 1920s, for Parliamentary approval was not granted until 1930. Contrary to beliefs expressed elsewhere, there was no correlation between the yard's construction and the MSW electrification; they were completely separate entities. As described, construction of the yard was a mammoth enterprise. Aside from the actual layout of the yard, the main line had to be diverted and there was the small matter of the removal of 1 1/4 *million* cubic yards of spoil; of this, around half a million cubic yards were required for embankments. The total length of the new yard was 1 1/3 miles. Another major work required was the reconstruction of the overbridge, known locally as "Gamesley Bridge", carrying the Glossop Road (A626) over the main line.

The accompanying two photographs, though not of the highest quality, give some idea of the scale and magnitude of the work being executed. The small excavator looks at odds with the size of such equipment seen at work today.

**(Top)** Contractors H.Arnold & Son used three Manning-Wardle-type 0-6-0s on the work for the new yard.Though not readily identifiable, two are clearly visible here. Looking east, the viaduct spanning the site and carrying the Glossop Road can be seen in the far background in both photographs.

**(Centre)** This was one one of three Atkinson-Walker vertical boiler locos used by Arnold & Son on the Mottram yard contract. Dating from 1930, all three (Nos.117-119) were supplied new to the company. *Both - Author's collection*

**(Left) May 29th 1937:** Mottram yard was only some two years old when Mr.Pollard called at the site with his Goerz-Anschütz reflex quarter-plate camera. B17 No.2845 *The Suffolk Regiment* speeds past the yard with the Liverpool-Harwich Boat train (the so-called "North Country Continental"). Recalling an earlier picture on Gorton shed, note the coal in the tender piled high almost to the limits of the loading gauge. Though only partially visible, the photograph gives some idea of the size and spaciousness of the yard.
*R.D.Pollard/Manchester Loco Society*

## Three views showing traffic in and around the yard

**(Left) May 29th 1937:** Ex-NER Class B15 4-6-0 of York shed is seen in the reception sidings at the head of a lengthy train of wagons. Two shunters, one equipped with an uncoupling pole, appear to be paying attention to the top of the train. The driver, adorned in typical cloth cap, casts a backward glance as he receives instructions.

*R.D.Pollard/Manchester Loco Society*

**(Centre) May 31st 1950:** Into the post-War era era with 04/7 No.63770 belonging to Hull (Dairycoates), one of the rebuilt GC 2-8-0s with a shortened 02 boiler, standing on one of the reception roads with a Down freight at 11.05 am. Notice the embankment in the background carrying the main line, busy as ever with yet more freight. The view gives some idea of the size and exposed nature of the yard. Working conditions here in winter must have been atrocious. Alas, that was life on the railway.

*R.D.Pollard/Manchester Loco Society*

**(Left) May 31st 1950:** Though preparations for electrification are looming large now, we are still firmly rooted in the steam era as Gorton B1 No.61184 clears the Glossop Road overbridge with the 9.30 am Liverpool Central to Hull express. Notice the newly-built section of the bridge where the yard passes beneath. Photographers Messrs. Pollard and Fields were present here on the same day and at roughly the same time. But did they ever meet? Our Hull express was due in the East Coast port city at 2.16 pm.

*Neville Fields/Mcr Loco Society*

## The Waterside branch

As mentioned earlier, the original station at Dinting dated from 1845. A more permanent structure was opened in 1847. This lasted until the early 1880s when, using the MS&L Railway (Additional Powers) Act of 1883, the company doubled the branch to Glossop and provided in addition an east to south curve connecting the Glossop branch over to the main line. At the same time the platforms were enlarged and rebuilt and new station buildings were erected. Dinting's early station had been sited some ¾ mile nearer to Manchester on the west side of the Dinting Vale viaduct. When the later station opened on the viaduct's opposite side, the early station was renamed "Old Dinting" and was retained solely for goods traffic.

It is from this point that we take a brief look away from Dinting before we travel further east towards Hadfield. From Old Dinting a branch some 2 ¼ miles long was constructed. Known as The Waterside Branch, the line served the Mersey Mills, the River Etherow Bleach Works and the Waterside Mill complex close to the River Etherow and lying between Hadfield and Tintwistle. An Act of 1874 enabled construction and the line opened for traffic in 1879. Owned by Gartside & Company, the Waterside mills were engaged in the traditional industries associated with this part of Derbyshire: the production of cotton and calico cloth. Leaving Old Dinting the branch was steeply graded (at 1-in-40) in order to cross the Glossop to Marple road. The line then crossed the valley on a trestle viaduct close to the site of the Roman Fort of Melandra Castle. The run-down of UK cloth production, coupled with the rapid encroachment of road transport ensured the demise of the Waterside branch. It was cut back by around one mile in 1962 before closure for good in 1965.

**Waterside Branch, May 2nd 1959:** As was ever the case, lines and stations threatened with closure were frequently visited by enthusiasts' specials; all those on board doubtless keen to "have done the branch", or such similar speak, before closure was effected. On a fine spring day an excellent panorama of Dinting Vale presents itself as BR Standard 2-6-4 tank No.80044 brings an REC Special over the spindly viaduct crossing Cottage Lane and on towards Gartside's Mill. Melandra Castle lies just behind the photographer.
*Keith Thompson*

**Woolleybridge, Waterside Branch, June 18th 1951:** At Woolleybridge, just below Hadfield, the Waterside Branch crossed the Woolleybridge Road via a level crossing to reach the Mersey cotton mills seen here on the left. In this picture the crossing gates are being dutifully closed after the arrival of Gorton's N5 0-6-2 tank No.69353. A few hundred yards further along, at the top of the long siding, the branch split to form two sets of sidings; one crossed the Etherow to serve the Bleach works, the other to serve the Mersey Mills. After the closure of the branch the crossing gates hung in situ for some years before being purchased by a local garden centre as a feature for their railway! *British Railways*

**Dinting viaduct in modern times:** Winter 1954 and towards the last days of steam: a B1 crosses the viaduct and heads west with an 8-coach (plus van) express. The west-side bricked-up arches and later strengthening piers are clearly visible. The A57 road runs beneath the structure alongside the house and the poster boards in the middle foreground. *B.K.B.Green*

## DINTING - CHANGE FOR GLOSSOP CENTRAL

To most enthusiasts the name Dinting is synonymous with two things: the steam preservation centre – The Dinting Railway Centre- run by the Bahamas Locomotive Society and active from1969 through to 1991 and the adjacent viaduct. Though always known to locals as "The Dinting Arches", its correct historical title is "Dinting Vale Viaduct". Almost immediately after passing the site of Mottram yard the railway encounters a void in the shape of Dinting Vale. Regarded by most people as a box girder structure sitting on a mixture of stone and brick piers, this is not the true picture of the viaduct by any means. Dinting viaduct is comprised of three separate components: working east from Mottram yard is a series of seven stone arches, each 50ft.wide and 22ft.10in.between the parapets. Sitting in the middle – "the viaduct" to most observers – is the central section made up from five openings (later divided by strengthening piers). A further series of four stone arches, again, each 50ft.wide, takes the railway to a westerly junction with the Glossop branch and into Dinting station. As at Mottram, the original superstructure was built from wood resting on stone piers; ships carpenters from Ireland are known to have been recruited for the works. The contract for the Dinting viaduct was let to Buxton & Clarke in September 1842 for the tendered sum of £31,600.

### Dinting Vale viaduct – a thumbnail sketch

Though substantially built in the first instance, within ten to twelve years after erection, the timber in both the Dinting and Mottram viaducts had decayed to such an extent as to pose a risk as to their safety. The MS&L consulted with their resident engineer, Alfred Jee whose solution was to truss the structures diagonally with iron rods to prevent bulging. However, by 1858 the viaducts were again in such a state as to alarm both passengers and local residents; passengers are reported to have been driven several miles to avoid crossing either bridge. A contemporary report states that the timberwork in part of the Mottram Viaduct was deflected downwards by some three to four inches during the passage of a train! Indeed, so serious was the problem that the railway company seriously considered using omnibuses (then horse-drawn of course) between to the two points in order to by-pass the viaducts.

At this period in history the development of wrought-iron for railway bridges had been exemplified in the construction of the Chester & Holyhead Railway. The building of this line had thrown up serious challenges to Robert Stephenson, the line's engineer in the form of necessary structures to bridge the Conwy Estuary and the Menai Straits. Stephenson had favoured bridges supported by chains. Enter at this juncture, the renowned 19th century engineer, Sir William Fairbairn, Bart. Fairbairn had experimented with tubular girders in the form of rectangular boxes at his Poplar works at Millwall, London. The result was Stephenson's acceptance of Fairbairn's ideas and thus was born the Conwy and Britannia (Menai Straits) tubular bridges.

History has not been kind to Fairbairn. For writers invariably invoke Stephenson when referring to the bridges described. Indeed, the author was guilty of a similar offence when he was introduced to one of Fairbairn's ancestors a few years ago. A short lecture followed by some lengthy reading of Fairbairn's biography ensued; his studies were completed by reference to papers dated February 24th 1862 and held in the archives of the Institution of Civil Engineers (ICE).

Fairbairn had been consulted by the MS&L as to the best way of reconstructing the two viaducts using some form of iron. Falling on his achievements in North Wales, he suggested the use of his favoured wrought-iron tubular girders. The company accepted Fairbairn's designs, but made one important stipulation: while the renewal work was being undertaken, the traffic should not be interrupted during the progress of the works. Given that there were some seventy trains per day passing over the viaducts, this was not a stipulation to be taken lightly.

Fairbairn, ever the practical engineer, came up with a solution. The replacement girders would be constructed on top of the old existing platforms and the stone side piers and abutments would be cut down. Then, by means of a simple screw apparatus, the girders would be suspended at each end and lowered into position. The ICE paper records that: no stoppage (of trains), even of a single minute, occurred, and that the whole of the work was accomplished without accident. Also mentioned is the fact that Fairbairn: was ably and cheerfully assisted by the Company's Engineer, Mr.Charles Sacré, and to that gentleman he is indebted for many useful suggestions.

Fairbairn's structures proved extremely sound. The Dinting girders were strengthened with steel in 1894 and the intermediate brick piers, seven in all, were added between 1918-20. Spanning a total width of 1200 feet, just over half of this is taken up by the central section (openings nos.8-12); maximum headway under the girders is recorded variously as between 119-130ft. Dinting viaduct's cross girders were renewed in 1939 and the line across was singled in 1977 to ease the loadings.

As this manuscript is completed (June 2013) Network Rail are completing an extensive programme of refurbishment to the Dinting viaduct. That at Mottram was similarly completed in 2011. Doubtless, when the first fare-paying passengers made what must have seemed like a perilous journey over the viaducts, they found the view breathtaking. That, some 170 years later, passengers in the 21st century can partake of the same experience, is a tribute indeed to the civil engineers' work spanning three centuries.

## Dinting station

The first station here, sited immediately to the east of the viaduct, opened as plain "Glossop" on 24th December 1842. When the Duke of Norfolk's Glossop branch opened – on 9th June 1845 – the station became known as "Dinting"; the station at the end of the Duke's branch becoming known as "Glossop" at the same time. Just to confuse matters Dinting itself became "Glossop AND Dinting some time before 1922. The same year "Glossop" became "Glossop Central", presumably to avoid confusion with the station on the main line. British Railways had the last word when, in May 1978, they renamed the place to just plain "Glossop". Dinting in 1922 had become "Dinting change for Glossop Central". Plain "Dinting" was substituted in BR days, but exactly when is not known.

**(Below) Dinting Vale, June 30th 1949**:An evening view, around 8.00, looking south-east across to Dinting station and the viaduct with the town of Glossop lying behind. Crossing the viaduct is B1 No.61152 with an Up express goods, probably ex-Deansgate or Ducie Street. We leave our train to pass along towards Hadfield with the summer clouds high over Whitely Nab and Cown Edge, finishing our evening with a leisurely walk and maybe a "pint" or two in "The Grouse" or "The Hare and Hounds". *Harold.D.Bowtell/Manchester Loco Society*

## Three views at Dinting station

**(Top) 1937:** The station in a quiet moment. A view looking north along the main line from below the central island platform. The Glossop branch veers off to the right, while the (then) main line due north to Hadfield swings away to the left. A train for Glossop is about to leave by the looks of things; the ensemble being made up of the 6-wheeled coaches that have become quite familiar since we left London Road. Peeping out just beyond the Dinting Road overbridge is the little hut (*qv*) that did duty for the S&T department here. There is much MS&L/GCR interest in this view: the platform mounted signalbox on the Down main line platform; the GCR lower-quadrant semaphores with Distants beneath for Mottram No.2 box; the lattice footbridge and those splendid gas lamps once again. A lone figure, a railwayman, complete with waistcoat, collar and tie, seems determined to make his mark on the picture; he succeeded!

*Lens of Sutton collection/Roger Carpenter*

**(Centre) June 16th 1950:** To most enthusiasts it was the Robinson freight engines – the O4s and the Q4s - that typified steam over Woodhead. Though this is to large degree true, the North Eastern locos also put in appearances in quite significant numbers. An archivist in the Manchester Loco Society has recorded some 220. With these statistics in mind it was good to come across this splendid shot of ex-NER Class Q6 No.63436 belonging to Selby (50C) drifting into the station with a Down freight train. Notice the nameboard (LNER-pattern on concrete posts) "DINTING CHANGE FOR GLOSSOP CENTRAL". The Up Home signal is "pegged off" for the main line towards Hadfield. The arm on the left is for a loop that ran off beyond the overbridge. This bracket signal betrays some GC ancestry: the curved cast-iron supporting bracket, whilst the keen-eyed may have noted the GC finial on the main post (an LNER cap sits on the branch post). Such simple detective work proves that the loop was a post-GCR addition and another example of how the expanding Woodhead freight traffic was managed piecemeal.

*Neville Fields/Manchester loco Society*

**(Lower) c.1930s:** The photographer is stood at the Manchester end of the island platform to capture B3 4-6-0 No.6169 *Lord Faringdon* about to depart with a Down express. Beyond the obligatory trespass and line crossing warning there would later be displayed a sternly-worded sign to railway personnel warning them not to use the viaduct as a walkway to Mottram yard. Sound advice; it was a long way down into Dinting Vale! *Author's collection*

**(Top) c.1946/47:** C1 Atlantic No.2885 rounds the curve from the Glossop Branch and on towards Hadfield. Then allocated to Doncaster, there is no record of why this engine was at Dinting at the time. One of a mere handful of C1s to survive into 1950 (aside from the preserved No.251). No.2885 was withdrawn in January of that year.

*Eric Oldham*

**(Lower) September 15th 1934:** C4 Atlantic No.5358 enters Dinting with the 12.15pm express from Marylebone. Then a Leicester engine – the traditional change-over point for engines and men on the London trains – appearances of the C4s over Woodhead were by then becoming rarer; the class having been supplanted on these trains by the "Directors" and the "Footballers".

*R.D.Pollard/Manchester Loco Society*

**(Top) Dinting: August 24th 1935:** Caprotti-fitted B3 No.6168 *Lord Stuart of Wortley* presents a clear exhaust against the backdrop of a summer sky as it clears Dinting station and lifts the 5.00 pm express from Manchester London Road to Cleethorpes along the 1-in-100 towards Hadfield. The 5-coach train comprised of former GCR vehicles would give way later in the decade to LNER Gresley stock. Whether either of these formations would be preferable to a similar journey today (though not, of course, over Woodhead) via First TransPennine Express is a moot point.

**(Centre)** On the same day Mr.R.D.Pollard re-loaded his plate camera, bequeathing to us this powerful shot. C1 Atlantic No.4434, then a Neepsend engine, bears down on him at the head of a Liverpool to Hull express. Notice the crew member leaning from the engine as if about to shout a warning. With the tripod perched close to the ballast shoulder, mortal danger was a mere couple of feet away. Unthinkable today, but such intrepid behaviour was par for the course in days gone by.

**(Lower) May 31st 1939:** Approaching Dinting from the east is B17 No.2864 *Liverpool* with the 12.15 express from Marylebone. Overall journey time for the London trains back then was in the region of 5¼ hours. In the early years of the GC "The Sheffield Special" had managed the journey in 4 hours and 10 minutes. However, over 20 years previously the GN/MS&L Joint express workings were completing the King's Cross to Manchester run in an even 5 hours.

*All three pictures - R.D.Pollard/Manchester Loco Society*

## Leaving Dinting for Hadfield

**(Top) September 15th 1934:** Mr.Pollard has positioned himself along bridge No.58 to catch No.2816 *Fallodon* roaring away from Dinting and heading towards Hadfield with the "North Country Continental", the fabled "Boat Train" that was such a feature of the Woodhead line. The appearance of *Fallodon* on this train is particularly apt as this engine was one of the first B17s to appear at Gorton in 1931*, along with sister engine No.2834 *Hinchingbrooke*; marking a sea-change in the working of "The Continental". The Dinting to Hadfield loop, mentioned earlier, continues on the right-hand side of the picture. Mr.Pollard's vantage point is Shaw Lane, the thoroughfare leading to Mouselow Quarry. In the LNER bridge register the road is listed as "Marlow Brow".
**both were still at Gorton when this picture was taken*

**(Centre) August 17th 1935:** Almost a year on and now working down at track-level with his tripod positioned in the middle of the Up loop (!), Mr.Pollard opens his shutter as O4 No.6268 (ex-N.B.Loco No.1868) slogs past with a Godley to Wath yard coal empties. With steam brake only on the loco and hand-braked, loose-coupled wagons, this was freight train operation at its most basic.

**(Lower) May 31st 1939:** As mentioned earlier, fish traffic was of enormous importance to the GCR; Robinson having built both locomotives and rolling stock especially to handle it. B7 No.5034 works hard as it darkens the sky with the 3.00 pm Ashburys to Grimsby fish empties. Come August and Mr.Pollard would put away his camera for five years before treating us to any more of his classic shots.

**All:** *R.D.Pollard/Manchester Loco Society*

**Dinting loco shed, c.1947:** The caption to our front cover recalled that the name of Dinting was synonymous with the west side of the Woodhead line. Here is a view that will recall for those enthusiasts lucky enough to have known the Dinting Railway Centre, one of the site's key landmarks – the famous single-road engine shed that stood just in front of the main building, home to so many of the locos that were once based there. The photographer has the viaduct behind him and is looking north-east across the station complex and towards Dinting Road.

*J.D.Darby/Manchester Loco Society*

## GLOSSOP

The town was once part of "Glossopdale" – a collection of villages clustered around Glossop Brook, a tributary of the River Etherow. A reminder of this exists today with "Old Glossop" still in use as a reference to the actual village. The town's ancestry lay in woollen milling which soon gave way to cotton and its associated cloth – Calico. Not that this was the only industry here: a gas works and iron foundry existed to the east and west of Shrewsbury Street, off the High Street and close to the station. St.Luke's church, close to Spire Hollin, the Unitarian and Methodist chapels all reflected the varying religious beliefs of the one-time mill owners. Another form of railway once served Glossop: running along the A57 road from the Hyde direction was the Glossop tramway. Commencing outside the Queen's Hotel in Old Glossop, the electric system was inaugurated in August 1903 linking Glossop with neighbouring Hadfield; though the 4-mile route was isolated from the surrounding networks of Stockport, Manchester, Hyde and Stalybridge. The tracks headed west out of the town along Glossop High Street with a short branch leading from the Town Hall down to the gates of Whitfield Lodge on Charlestown Road, home of Sir John Wood. Glossop's trams ceased operation on Christmas Eve, 1927.

Returning to the beginnings of the railway: Glossop received its line by courtesy of the Duke of Norfolk in June 1845 when the one-mile branch, built and owned by His Grace, opened for passengers. Though running over the Duke's own land – something that obviated the need for an Act of Parliament – the branch was operated from the start by the SAuL&M/MS&L, though the Duke's family – the Howards – had their own private entrance to Glossop station. The line was built originally in a trailing direction from the Sheffield direction. As referred to in the Dinting section, a connecting curve just west of the latter was opened in 1884 completing the arrangement which survives today. And we saw earlier in this volume how the branch was worked by ex-GCR Class F1 and F2 2-4-2 tanks which ran a service from Manchester London Road coupled to rakes of ten 6-wheeled coaches. In the early years of WWII bogie stock was introduced and the redoubtable C13 4-4-2 tanks arrived to replace the aged 2-4-2s. As mentioned, seven of the C13s were push-pull (or "motor-fitted") and these worked the two-coach units, one of which had the distinction of carrying an ex-GCR 12-wheeled saloon carriage.

One of the highlights of the service came when working the 5.17 pm (later 5.20) Manchester-Glossop push-pull which pushed two coaches and had one extra put on to the rear. The train was non-stop to Newton and was very popular with local users rejoicing in the unofficial title of "The Glossop Express".

Tony Quirke, who began his railway career at Gorton works, recalls the train thus: *"The Glossop push-pull invariably swept past Hyde Junction as were alighting from the 5.03 pm from London Road to Marple and, even though it was only given ten minutes non-stop to Guide Bridge, it was actually passing Hyde Junction just thirteen minutes after leaving Manchester!"*

Sited at the east end of the town the small terminal station backs on to Norfolk Street with Henry Street, Howard Street, Charles Street and Fitzalan Street close by - all names associated with Glossop's historical past and the Duke of Norfolk's promotion of the short branch. One final connection with the railway worthy of a mention is the football and cricket grounds that stand on the north side of the line. Here is the home of Glossop North End. The team rose to national fame in May 2009 when they played Whitley Bay for the FA Vase at Wembley. Though losing 2-1, the supporters had the distinction of travelling on what was the only express to leave Glossop station (certainly for London) for many years!

**(Top) Glossop Central, c.1956:** Lovely day for a Guinness at Glossop Central! This is the station frontage photographed from along Norfolk Street. A golden lion, symbolic beast of the Howard family, stands astride the left-hand station entrance. This was the Howard family's own private entrance. A BRITISH RAILWAYS maroon totem above the right-hand entrance draws passengers' attention to "Cheap Trips" – priced at 11/- on offer from Glossop to Leicester on Sunday 6th November. *C.H.A.Townley*

**(Centre) September 2nd 1950:** The rural aspects of the Derbyshire market town form a backdrop to this scene as C13 4-4-2 tank No.67438 heads away from Glossop and passes along to Dinting. Despite the encroaching signs of electrification, steam will have almost four years of life here yet.

**(Lower)** On the same day, photographer Neville Fields has moved back down to the station to give us this fine overview of the proceedings. With No.67438 again as the motive power, the push-pull set waits to leave the station's island platform; the goods yard is off to the right. Notice the first carriage, a GC clerestory of early 1900s vintage (qv the picture of the local at Wilbraham Road) with the saloon coach behind. The tall building at right-angles to the station is a Wesleyan chapel and Sunday school. Further motive power can be glimpsed down by the buffer stops in the shape of a J11 0-6-0.

**Both:** *Neville Fields/ Manchester Loco Society*

**Glossop, September 2nd 1950:** Today is a Saturday and the usual arrangement at weekends was for J11s and N5s to take over the working of the Manchester to Glossop and Hadfield service at weekends while the C13s sojourned at Gorton for maintenance - boiler washouts etc. Typifying this arrangement J11 No.64322 leaves Glossop with a return service. The summer 1950 timetable shows seventeen weekday trains serving Glossop and Hadfield in and out of Manchester London Road. A further five were designated as Saturdays only. And though most trains called at Glossop before reversing and going on to Hadfield, a number terminated at Glossop before returning directly back to Manchester. One exception to this was the fabled 5.20 pm from London Road, as well as the 8.01 pm and 10.25 pm from Manchester, both trains Saturdays only. *Neville Fields/Manchester Loco Society*

## Push-pull workings, a footnote (with thanks to Tony Quirke)

Dinting shed, run by a driver-in-charge, regularly manned a push-pull fitted C13 on the Glossop-Manchester service and it was a requirement that the fireman had to be a passed driver. In 1952 the Dinting C13 left Gorton shed at 2.55 am and worked the 4.25 newspaper train to Marple using the two push-pull coaches to carry the papers in. The loco then worked the 5.00 am Marple to Manchester local running as a push-pull after which it worked to 5.45 morning push-pull from London Road to Glossop to start the day's push-pull operations from there. The loco was triple manned throughout its diagram, returning to Gorton shed at 11.30 pm after covering 175 miles in 20 hours!

## HADFIELD

"A good pedigree" would be a suitable phrase to apply to Hadfield and its surrounding lands. Owners through the centuries have included William the Conqueror, Kings Henry I, II & VIII, The Earl of Shrewsbury and, latterly, The Duke of Norfolk. Crossing this noble terrain the Great Central main line cuts in from the bottom of the map – a short distance along from neighbouring Dinting. Passing under Marlow Brow, Hadfield station is encountered; notice the footbridge, the large goods shed and ample siding provision – all reflecting the high level of freight traffic here once upon a time.

The SAuL&M opened for business at Hadfield on 7th August 1844. The suffix "For Hollingworth" lasted until modern times when the place became just plain "Hadfield". Hollingworthhall Moor and the Hollingworth (Swallows Wood) nature reserve lie to the north-west of the station. Hadfield's station buildings were to a typical MS&L style. Like others on this stretch of railway, they offered substantial structures on one side, with more rudimentary, but still quite stylish, accommodation on the other. Today, Hadfield's Down building has long gone; that on the Up side remains, though part is in use as nowadays as a wine bar. The station's goods shed survives – though much extended - as a warehouse for Messrs.Ashton Steels.

At Hadfield, not be confused with neighbouring Padfield, the Woodhead line entered the Longdendale Valley where, to quote one writer, the landscape comprises "water, moors and sky". Here, the vast chain of reservoirs built for Manchester Corporation between 1854 and 1877 by the redoubtable pioneer and water engineer, John Frederick La Trobe Bateman (1810-1899), stretch out as far as the eye can see. Beginning with the smaller Arnfield reservoir, the line is fringed by the chain as it proceeds on to Bottoms, Valehouse, Rhodeswood, Torside and Woodhead reservoirs before being swallowed whole by the famous tunnel.

**Hadfield, September 12th 1953:** To paraphrase a well-worn Americanism - *There's gold in them thar' mills* - or at least there was once. Evidence of Hadfield's cotton spinning past stands out in the background as O4 No.63573 drifts down towards the station with a loaded (Down) coal train. This is steam's last full year of operation – over 100 years and how many coal trains? The siding on the far left served the coal drops here. Beyond is reservoir territory with Padfield main road spanning the railway in the distance.

*Gordon Coltas Photo Trust*

**Hadfield, August 17th 1946:** Class O1 No.3886 stands in the Up sidings with no less than four railwaymen posing for Doug Darby's camera. Emerging from Gorton just two weeks beforehand, the loco had been rebuilt from a Class 04/3 with a B1 boiler and new cylinders. Built originally by the North British Loco Co. in 1919, the engine became surplus to requirements and was stored before purchase by the LNER in September 1928. Allocated to Gorton for all of its two lives under the LNER, the engine was moved to Annesley in October 1950 from where it was withdrawn in October 1962.

*J.D.Darby/Manchester Loco Society*

Looking away from Hadfield station, more prominent than anything else here was the sight of Station Mill, the large complex built in 1834 by Thomas and Edward Platt to the north-west of the main line. Here, in a nutshell, was what the town's industry was all about – the business of cotton, silk and Worsted cloth manufacture. East of the station were positioned coal drops providing the vital fuel for the town's mills. The drops were situated off Platt Street, a thoroughfare named after the aforementioned notable family who had been farmers in Longdendale for generations. Over the Padfield Main Road the ground quickly gives way to moorland before encountering Bottoms Reservoir. Spanning the line at the station is Marlow Brow; from there fans out a series of streets: Church Street, Railway Street and Marlow Street all with their neat terraced houses, homes of former mill workers and dwellings far removed from *The Thorns,* the mansion-style building close to the Old Quarry off Park Road. Hadfield today forms the terminus of the severed Woodhead line; alighting from his train the traveller sees the sign pointing to the Longdendale Trail, a long-distance footpath allowing cyclists, walkers and horse riders the freedom of the Dark Peak stretching out into yonder wilderness. It is at this point that we complete our journey out from London Road, travelling back in time to explore another important facet of the Woodhead line: the minor, but nonetheless important terminus of Manchester Central.

**(Top) Approaching Hadfield from Dinting, c.1930s:** K2 Mogul No.4660, a Colwick engine and a class not that common over Woodhead, runs alongside the Up loop with a train comprised of vans and sheeted wagons. *W.Oliver*

**(Centre) Hadfield station December 28th 1948:** In the final days of BR's first year, green-liveried B1 No.61317 replete with white headcode discs charges through the station with an Up express. The view shows off well the handsome lines of the station's architecture. Notice the stone ornaments complete with ball finials in similar fashion to those down the line at Newton. *Neville Fields/Manchester Loco Society*

**(Lower) Hadfield station, 1953:** A view looking north-eastwards away from the station and on towards Valehouse and Torside. Drifting cautiously along the 1-in-100 downgrade is an unidentifiable O4 with a loaded coal train. The photographer has caught nicely the outline of the Down side platform shelter, compare this with that at Newton. Alongside this building the poster board is still headed **"LONDON & NORTH EASTERN RAILWAY";** the right-hand poster is one of the now forgotten temporary BR totems – the familiar white outline reading **"HADFIELD"** set against a dark blue background. A real rarity at one of today's Railwayana auctions perhaps? *Norman Harrop*

**Manchester Central, c.1934/35:** The magnificent arched roof of the terminus dominates the view - typifying the use of the station by the Boat trains that plied the Woodhead line is this rare view of Pollitt D6 4-4-0 No.5863 pulling away from platform 2 with the Liverpool-bound Harwich Boat Train – "The Continental" to one and all. The coach destination boards (three per roof) on this celebrated express read: (1) "LIVERPOOL & MANCHESTER; (2) HARWICH PARKESTON QUAY (3) CONTINENTAL EXPRESS". In the 1930s the train ran to two distinct timetables: one for Tuesdays, Wednesdays and Thursdays, the other for Mondays, Fridays and Saturdays. The former working carried a restaurant car from Harwich through to York. On Tue/Wed/Thu the train left Harwich (PQ) at 7.25 am, called at Ipswich at 8.06, Ely at 9.35, March 10.00, Spalding 10.26, Sleaford 10.51 and Lincoln 11.20. Due in Sheffield Victoria at 12.42, "The Continental" crossed the Pennines to arrive in Manchester Central at 1.55. Reversal took place (as seen here) with arrival due in Liverpool Central at 2.43 pm. The coaches then formed the Up 4.00 Liverpool to Hull train, returning the following morning from Hull to Liverpool in time for the east-bound "Continental". Notice the signalbox – the "B" cabin - on the right-hand side of the view and the lower quadrant CLC signals, all soon to be swept away by the power re-signalling scheme of 1935. *William Lees*

## MANCHESTER CENTRAL & THE MS&L/GCR

### The station described

The MS&L's association with this latterday Manchester terminus came about by the company's joint tenure, along with the Midland and the Great Northern railway companies, of the Cheshire Lines Committee (CLC). Mooted initially under an Act of Parliament dated July 13th 1863, the legislation enabled the GNR and the MS&L to operate in tandem a number of existing concerns. A further Act – The Cheshire Lines Transfer Act, dated July 5th 1865, enabled incorporation of the Midland Railway. Fully fledged in July 1866, the CLC retained its independence until Nationalisation in 1948, usually referring to themselves as "The Cheshire Lines Railway". The conglomerate possessed no locomotives of its own, motive power being provided by the MS&L/GCR although the CLC did build its own coaching stock.

Costing £14,000, the first Manchester Central station had two platforms, 500 and 600 feet long respectively. The platform roads were interspersed with two tracks between them. An all-over roof covered the ensemble. June 26th 1877 saw the first train entering the new station, with the public opening coming on July 9th. Waxing lyrical, The Manchester Guardian described the new station as……a beautiful substantial building, the waiting rooms of which were elegantly decorated, and reflected great credit on the task of those who had the direction of the works. After the station's eclipse-when the new terminus opened-this first station was converted to goods use and opened for business on December 1st 1880, five months after the new station saw its first trains. By March 1883 its capacity had been extended by the addition of two wagon hoists to convey traffic to and from the station undercrofts. Goods facilities at Central were extended by an impressive 3-storey goods warehouse which stood in front and to the side of the station along Windmill Street and Watson Street.

But the first station was small and had only been intended as a stop-gap before greater things would emerge. Indeed, the work on the larger edifice was well under way, a start having been made in October 1875. Central's design has been erroneously attributed to Sir John Fowler. However, the design was the product of H.L.Moorson who was appointed by the CLC as Resident Engineer for the Central project in 1872. Moorson's drawings are signed by Charles Sacré, R.Johnson and A.Johnstone-respectively Engineers of the MS&L, the GN and the Midland railways. The contract for approach tracks to the station from Cornbrook as far as Great Bridgewater Street was awarded to Edward Johnson in January 1873. Alas, the author's namesake died in 1877 before his task could be completed. A new contract went to Messrs.Kirk & Parry who completed the job. Johnson's contract, along with that of Eastwood, Swingler & Co. who constructed the viaducts over the wharves and canal at Castlefield, cost the CLC a total of £106,204-8/-3d.

***(continued on page 132.......)***

**Manchester Central, March 15th 1899:** Polished to perfection and watched by a crowd of admiring onlookers, GNR Class D1 4-4-0 No.1343 makes a lively start away from platform 6 with one of the inaugural Great Northern King's Cross expresses. This day, a Wednesday, saw the opening of the Great Central's London Extension and, clearly, the GN were out to match the competition! Six of H.A.Ivatt's "400" Class D1 (LNE D3) 4-4-0s were sent to Trafford Park shed (itself opened just four years earlier) to work these Manchester expresses. The train in our photograph could be either the 10.10 am or the 12.10 pm to King's Cross. All the Up expresses ran via Nottingham and some ran over the Midland's Manchester South District line via Stockport Tiviot Dale and Woodley to reach Godley Junction. Journey times were around 4 ½ hours with engines being changed at either Nottingham or Grantham.
*Author's collection*

The Manchester company of Robert Neill & Sons were awarded the contract for the brick undercrofts and associated work up to platform level; Neills having tendered for the sum of £124,778-7/-5d. The roof, designed as single arch, was 210 ft.wide and sat at a maximum height of 90 ft. above rail level. Doubtless inspired by the roof at St.Pancras, where a span of 240 ft. rose to a crown; something that marked the London terminal out from its northerly counterpart. Construction of Central's magnificent roof was contracted to Andrew Handyside & Company of Derby. Despite a lower tender by a local firm, Handyside's bid of £58,032.13.1d and signed on December 30th 1876, won the day. One can only ponder as to what one (old) penny - 1d - bought 129 years ago? As built, the station had seven platforms all housed within the splendid single-arched train shed. Under the supervision of its first Stationmaster, Mr.J.H.Bell, the new Manchester Central station opened for traffic on July 1st 1880. An extension, increasing the station's capacity by two platforms (Nos.8&9) was opened in 1906 on the south side alongside Lower Mosley Street.

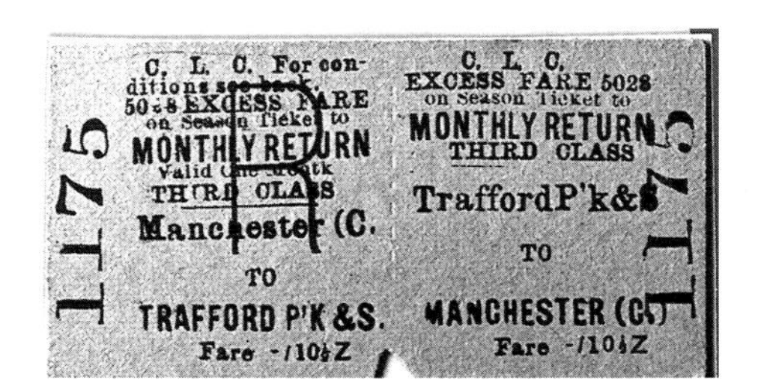


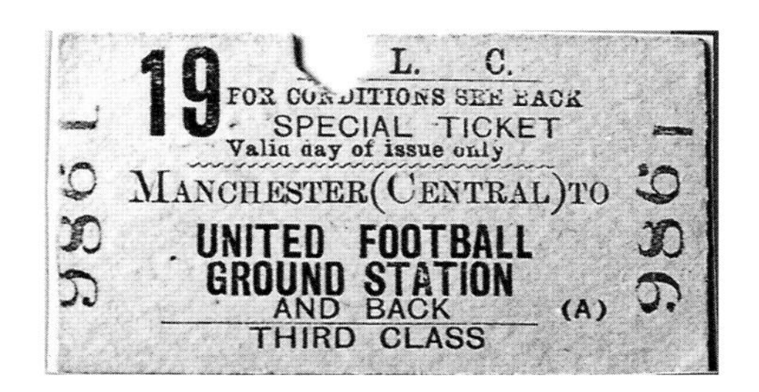

## Another route to London

It was not until the opening of the final section of the Manchester Central Station Railway ("The Fallowfield Line"), in May 1892, that Manchester Central, its passenger and goods facilities, were of any use to the MS&L as far as traffic over Woodhead goes. Some seven years later, when the GC extension to London opened - on March 15th 1899 - the Great Northern Railway by dint of its running powers over the GC (qv) began to work what had hitherto been joint expresses (with the MS&L) from King's Cross to Manchester, switching the terminus from London Road to Central in the process. GN interest in Manchester began on August 1st 1857 when the joint service with the MS&L commenced; two sidings at Ardwick were maintained by the company at this time (qv).

Later in the nineteenth century the GN's presence in Manchester had been strengthened greatly by the company's vast goods warehouse complex. Opened in 1897-98, this sat on a nine-acre site across from Central station along Watson Street and fronting along Deansgate. The use of Central station was forced on the GN as the company did not have running powers into Manchester London Road. An ambitious service of five trains each way was put on at first, but this declined quickly. Then, in July 1905, a creditable 4-hour service was instituted and in August next year a special luxury "Manchester" 4-coach set was put on - electrically-lit and vestibuled throughout; the stock being designed by none other than H.N.Gresley. But even the Edwardian monopoly of inland transport could not sustain such intense competition between the Capital and "Cottonopolis" and the GN's passenger service from Manchester Central gradually withered away, disappearing completely in the First War. Manchester was of course very well served with London expresses a hundred or so years ago: those over the GCR's new London Extension to Marylebone, as we have seen, operating largely out of London Road; the Midland's expresses from Central to St.Pancras and, finally, those over "The Premier Line" – the LNWR – from London Road to Euston. Alas, little or nothing has come to light photographically-speaking of either the Joint or the GN's own expresses during their passage over Woodhead; remarkable, despite their existence for well-nigh forty years or so.

The Manchester Central Station Railway gave the GCR another string to its bow when, in 1906, a connection of some 48 chains was made at Throstle Nest South Junction west to join the CLC's Manchester-Liverpool line at Trafford Park Junction. Via this chord, goods and passenger traffic could access Merseyside, avoiding Manchester Central. An interesting passenger working over the line occured c. 1927 when the morning Hull to Liverpool train briefly took this route instead of using Stockport Tiviot Dale and the Godley to Glazebrook line via Skelton Junction. The Throstle Nest chord enhanced the usefulness of the Woodhead line inasmuch as freight traffic from Merseyside, notably from Huskisson and Walton depots, could use the Fallowfield line to enable sorting at Dewsnap sidings, outside Guide Bridge (*qv*).

**Manchester Central, c.pre-WWI:** Gleaming from end to end and looking the very acme of perfection so typical of the period, GCR Class 8B (C4) Atlantic No.264 (Beyer, Peacock & Co.1904) waits to depart from platform 5 with an express, possibly for Marylebone. The loco is in entirely original condition: two whistles, Ramsbottom safety valves, side footsteps and cylinder tail rods; note, too, the original-pattern tender with coal rails. The elegant curved sides to the platform canopies are thought to have been straightened in the early 1930s to improve sighting in readiness for the power signalling scheme introduced in 1935. *P.F.Cooke*

**Manchester Central, c.1935-39:** "Is it a "Cop?" Although train spotting is considered to be a phenomenon of the immediate post-War period, here is evidence that this wonderful pastime was practised well before then. Very much the archetypal schoolboy of the period – clad in blazer, with cap, short trousers and long grey socks, our young man is seen dutifully recording the name and number of the subject of his study: "Sir Sam" No.5427 *City of London.* The fine LNER lined apple green livery and other detail differences make for interesting comparison with earlier views of these locos. So who was our mystery schoolboy standing on platform 8 around 76 years ago? Is he, perhaps, still with us? We will probably never know.

*Author's collection*

## Heyday of the GCR's expresses

Under Sir Sam Fay the GCR had made a speciality of through workings and in the 1920s Manchester Central was playing host to a summer through train to Yarmouth. Described in the timetable as a "Luncheon Corridor Express" the train left Manchester at midday and was due in Yarmouth (Vauxhall) at 5.56. Eric Dalton, records seeing the train hauled by "Sir Sam" 4-6-0s on two occasions in August 1924: No.426c "City of Chester" and No.5423 "Sir Sam Fay."

Southbound expresses over the former GCR main line via Sheffield, Leicester and London Marylebone were also seen at Central. From the opening of the London Extension, the station provided daily services to Nottingham, Leicester and Marylebone. Pre-War (1938) a train departed Central at 10.30 pm carrying newspapers and mail (having left Liverpool an hour earlier); on Sundays two Marylebone expresses were provided. One left at 12.15 pm, the other at 5.30 pm. Journey times were 5 hrs. 30 mins. and 4 hrs.50 mins. respectively.

Operating staff in the Manchester area always thought of the 3.20 pm Down express from Marylebone as the "crack" working of the day. Colloquially referred to as the "Sam Fay Down" the express was the successor to the "Sheffield Special", a train inaugurated by Sam Fay (as he then was) in 1903. The train was booked to leave Marylebone at 3.25 pm and ran non-stop to Sheffield, slipping coaches at Leicester and Penistone; journey time to Central was 4 hrs.10 mins. In the 1920s, as at London Road, GC "Directors" were superseding the "Sir Sam Fay" 4-6-0s and the GC Atlantics on the Marylebone turns. "Sams", though, were still seen coming into Central in on Hull and Leicester expresses until as late as 1938. From the mid-1930s the "Footballers" - B17s with LNER group standard tenders - augmented the "Directors" on these workings and on the Marylebone expresses. A mixture of J10 0-6-0s, N4 0-6-2 tanks and even ex-GN C12 4-4-2 tanks were deployed on local services from Central to Guide Bridge in the period up until the 1950s .

Away from Woodhead of course there was more to GC operations at Manchester Central than just the services mentioned here and elsewhere. From Central the GC ran its own services to Wigan (Central) and St.Helens, while the company provided motive power for the CLC's own route to Southport (Lord Street).

## Finale

Manchester Central closed to all traffic on May 3rd 1969 (Goods traffic had ceased in 1964 and the adjacent GNR goods warehouse had closed as long ago as 1954). The celebrated Harwich and Hull boat trains had been diverted over to Piccadilly since 1963, something that removed the last vestiges of links to former GC routes from here. After years of neglect the station was re-born in 1986 as "GMEX" and used as an exhibition and conference centre. From 2006 the site has once again become "Manchester Central". Today the Metrolink trams hum alongside the site of the old platforms 8 and 9 where once GC "Directors" arrived and departed with their trains to Chester. But all that, of course, is another part of railway history.

**Approaches to Manchester Central, c.1934/35:** The photographer has positioned himself on the brick-arched viaduct between Castlefield and Deansgate to give us this rare view of "The Continental" as it heads into the terminus prior to reversal for the next leg of the journey – onwards to Liverpool Central. The train is drawn by a C1 Atlantic, number unknown; the second coach is a GC "Matchboard" sandwiched in between two LNER teak-bodied Gresley vehicles. This was a period of transition for the terminus: notice the "X" on the new colour light signals just ahead of the loco. To the right, on the west side of Deansgate, is the station's "A" cabin soon to be made redundant. *William Lees*

**Manchester Central, c.1919-1922:** Apotheosis of the GCR 4-6-0: Robinson Class 9P No.1169 *Lord Faringdon* waits alongside platform 4 to depart, probably with a Marylebone express. The clarity of the photograph is remarkable, even the detail on the builder's plate is discernible. Clear, too, is the well-nigh immaculate condition of the loco – all steel and brasswork polished, right down to the covers of the Iracier axleboxes on the tender. Oh to be standing on Fallowfield station to watch her go through………. *P.F.Cooke*

**Boat trains pre and post-War: (Top) Mersey Road & Aigburth, c.1938:** En route to Manchester Central from Liverpool is Gorton's "Director" No.5511 *Marne* with an express bound for Hull. *J.Stone/Barry Allen collection*

**(Below) Spalding, July 7th 1951:** With B17 No.61635 *Milton* at its head, "The Continental" bound for Sheffield Victoria, waits to leave the station; the time will be around 10.55 am. At Sheffield the immaculate B17 will come off and a B1 will be waiting to take the train over Woodhead into Manchester Central. *J.P.Wilson*

**(Right) A section of a side-strip diagram from an LNER timetable of the mid-1930s**

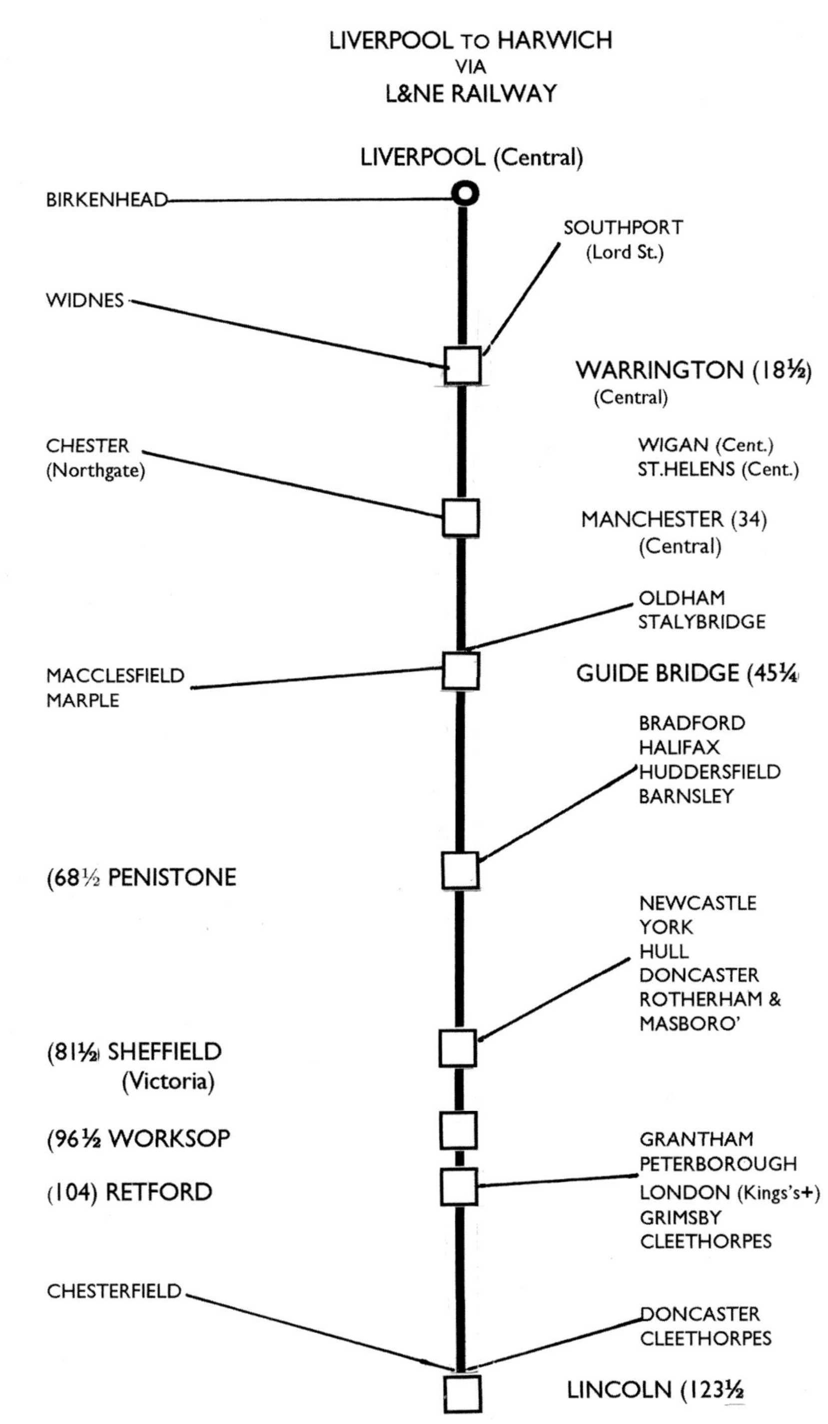

## Boat trains and cross-country services

The cross-country Boat trains from Harwich to Liverpool had their origins from 1885 when the GER began services from Harwich (Parkeston Quay) to York, later extended to the Midlands and the North of England. It was this train in one or other of its many modified workings that became known as the "North Country Continental." The GCR took over the workings from Lincoln and then via Sheffield to Manchester Central and Liverpool. After the First War restaurant cars were attached to the Manchester and Liverpool portions and it is in this period that the "Continental" achieved a measure of fame. As mentioned earlier, in 1927 ex-GER B12 4-6-0s began through working from Ipswich to Manchester, a turn taken over in 1929 by B17 "Sandringham" 4-6-0s with the Gorton and Ipswich men working through on alternate days. Through working from Ipswich into Manchester Central continued until 1941 when lodging turns from Gorton and Ipswich were abolished. One interesting sidelight on the various "Sandringham" workings was the use of the incoming engine on various local trains (qv). 4.25 pm local train to Guide Bridge - a treat for contemporary enthusiasts! In latter years the engine from the "Boat Train" completed its day's work by taking charge of the 7.22 evening train to Leicester. The LNER timetable for this period carries the stern reservation: *The Continental Express will not be held if the steamer is late in which event passengers holding tickets for Midlands and North may travel via London.* Clearly no fun, especially with luggage to carry!

**Woodley West, August 4th 1934**
At Woodley Junction the CLC line from Godley forked away south-west towards Stockport Tiviot Dale traversing Bredbury and Brinnington Junctions in the process. West of Woodley Junction was the small block post of Woodley West which appears to have been abolished before WWII. On a summer Saturday Mr.Pollard availed himself of a good viewpoint just outside Woodley West to give us these two fine views.

**(Top)** The route to Liverpool over this section of line was described in our caption of the C1 leaving Godley on page 109. Here is another Hull-Liverpool train, again Atlantic-hauled, this time by No.4434. The 7-coach train is the 2.50 pm from Hull and is augmented by two vans. Carrying a through portion for London Road (detached at Sheffield) the train was due in Stockport at 5.49, Glazebrook 6.08, Warrington Central 6.19 and Liverpool Central at 6.47.

**(Lower)** Taking the same route B7 No.5478 passes with a Bridlington to Liverpool special working. Notice the 7-coach formation has been strengthened by the addition of two 6-wheelers behind the tender. *Both: R.D.Pollard/ Manchester Loco Society*

Services to Hull had been established back in the nineteenth century, something unsurprising from a company with such strong maritime connections as the MS&L. Reference to the Hull workings appeared in our feature at Godley Junction where we noted the appearance of an ex-GN Class C1 Atlantic working over from Sheffield and via Woodhead into Manchester Central. The redoubtable C1s had first appeared in 1925 on the short-lived King's Cross-Manchester Pullman train via Retford and Sheffield. It is worth inserting here the only record that the author has ever seen concerning this long-lost train: a Manchester observer, Eric Dalton, noted the Up Pullman on August 20th 1925 was headed by C1 No.4421 with just one named car-Iolanthe-in the train. Returning to the C1s and the Hull Boat trains to and from Liverpool Central via Manchester Central: from 1929-39 these locomotives were deployed on what is referred to as a "Triangular (3-part) Diagram". Space precludes inclusion of all three of these, but here is one: 8.40 am Sheffield Victoria to Manchester Central to arrive at 9.57 am. 11.30 am Manchester Central to Liverpool Central to arrive at 12.15 pm. 1.18 pm Liverpool Central to Sheffield Victoria, travelling via Stockport Tiviot Dale. Our summary of services from Hull to Manchester and Liverpool has described several different routes, but there was one other.The LNER (GC section) summer excursion book for 1938 shows workings from both Hull and Cleethorpes (as well as Peterborugh) travelling over Woodhead, but then using the MSJ&A (GC & LNW Joint) section from London Road; calling also at Oxford Road the excurions ran via Cornbrook East Junction to gain the CLC main line and thence onwards to Liverpool Central via Glazebrook.
The section covering "Boat Trains" is completed by a reference- covered earlier - the services from Immingham to Manchester that ran in the summer in connection with the Orient Shipping Company's sailings to and from Norway.

## Journey's end

To complete this first part of our journey – "Steam Over Woodhead" – we travel just 3 ¼ miles from Manchester Central to the village of Chorlton-cum-Hardy. Immortalised by Flanders and Swann in their song "The Slow Train", the junction at "Chorlton" (as it has become nowadays) marked the end of the CLC's remit and the start of the Great Central and the Midland's own independent routes. From here the Midland's "Crimson Ramblers" and multifarious 4-4-0s hauling crimson coaches parted company with "Sams", "Directors" and "Sandringhams"; their teak-bodied counterparts strung out behind all ready for the slog up the bank past Fallowfield and on to Guide Bridge before heading out east over the iconic Woodhead route.

**(Top) Chorlton-cum-Hardy, c.mid-1920s:** Approaching the station is Class D9 4-4-0 No.5112 with a Down express. Ex-GCR services from Central included expresses to and from Cleethorpes, Hull and Yarmouth and the loco and coaching stock would suggest one of these within the period of the photograph.
*W.H. Whitworth*

**(Lower) Chorlton-cum-Hardy, c.early 1900s:** Looking the very epitome of the Edwardian suburban station, this was Chorlton seen over 100 years ago. The inlaid brickwork, fretted bargeboards and striped platform awnings were features all typical of CLC practice. A local train approaches alongside the Up platform drawn by a Midland 0-6-0 or 0-4-4 tank. The station lost its footbridge sometime before WWI. Rail services returned here in 2011 after an absence of over 44 years. Today the site houses a "Stop" on the newly extended Manchester Metrolink system.
*Collection of Graham Tickle*

**Chorlton-cum-Hardy station, c.mid-1930s:** A truly splendid study of Gorton's B17 No.2841 *Gayton Hall* seen in immaculate condition awaiting departure with a stopping train to Guide Bridge, exemplifying again the use of main line locomotives on Fallowfield line Locals, making economic use of both engine and men. Spanning the tracks is bridge No.15 taking Wilbraham Road in Chorlton village over the railway, 3 miles and 16 chains from Throstle Nest East Junction. In front, bridge No.16 carries a gas main belonging then to Manchester Corporation. Notice the loco crew leaning from the cab and casting a wary eye on the photographer!

*William Lees*

**Chorlton-cum-Hardy, April 1923:** This was Chorlton's bookstall, belonging to W.H.Smith and sited on the Down platform. The gentleman on the left is Reg Croton pictured with David Ball, the manager. 90 years ago the big story was the Royal wedding; the marriage of Lady Elizabeth Bowes-Lyon to Prince Albert George, the future King George VI. For the horticulturally-minded, Amateur Gardening (52 pages) offered features covering bedding plants, dahlia culture, melons and tomatoes – all for 2d!

*J.M.Lloyd collection/courtesy David Hadfield*

**Chorlton-cum-Hardy, n.d:** Taxi! Waiting in the station's forecourt is N 6122, a taxi with Reg Croton (on left) posing for the camera and David Ball. A good deal of middle-class housing surrounded the Chorlton district, so a "fare" was probably not that hard to come by. The vehicle is a Crossley car of a type manufactured (in Manchester) between 1908-1926; it has a modified body, notice the spilt windscreen and "Carbide" lamps. These used calcium carbide powder onto which was dripped water to produce acetylene gas. Another fine gas lamp can be seen on the station wall alongside a poster displaying an advert for railway advertising – contact Messrs.W.H.Blyth & Sons. A Morrisons supermarket covers the ground here today.

*J.M.Lloyd collection/courtesy David Hadfield*

**Chorlton-cum-Hardy station, 1913:** A photo call for the station staff just one hundred years ago shows 11 men assembled in front of the camera on the Down platform. We can safely assume that the gentleman standing in front of the "C" in "Cum" and sporting a double-breasted coat and winged collar is the Stationmaster. The number of staff may seem high, but with something like 60 trains per day calling here, as well as goods traffic to deal with, then there was plentiful employment for all, especially in those far-off days when labour was cheap. On a sombre note, one wonders how many of these men returned safely from the horrors of the First World War? *J.M.Lloyd collection/courtesy David Hadfield*

**Chorlton-cum-Hardy, 1926**: Approaching the station with an Up express from Manchester Central is the celebrated locomotive No.5423 *Sir Sam Fay*. The identity of the train is unsure, but by the looks of the mixed nature of the coaching stock – which includes two of the famous 6-wheelers – the train may well be bound for Cleethorpes or one of the East Coast resorts. Notice the goods shed to the left of the picture. The bridge in the background carries Stamford Road (today's Brantingham Road) over the railway. Users of the present-day Metrolink might find the scene depicted here something of a contrast with that of today!
*L.M.Hobdey*

**Chorlton-cum-Hardy, c.1949:** As we saw in our first features, the redoubtable mixed-traffic B7 locos were running on borrowed time in the period immediately after Nationalisation. Only two received their BR numbers and the class was extinct in early 1950. Looking grimy and unidentifiable, one of the locos fitted with the later pattern of cylinders (cf No.E1380 at Ardwick on p.19) pounds through the station with a train of coal empties, probably en route from Trafford Park sidings to Dewsnap. Notice the CLC-pattern lower-quadrant signal at the end of the Down platform and the wall-mounted gas lamp opposite; both specimens from the station's early years.
*W.A.Brown*

**Chorlton-cum-Hardy, August 1928:** The sight of a B12 in Manchester is a rare event, let alone one hauling a goods train! No.8573 was the third of a batch of ten of the very successful ex-GER 4-6-0s built for the LNER by Beyer, Peacock & Co.in 1928 (see caption p.42). No.8573 was ex-works from Beyers on August 27th 1928. Despite the poor quality of the picture, the immaculate condition suggests the loco was running in on a local trial before entering traffic proper. Our engine spent a short time at Gorton before heading down to London to its allocated shed, at Stratford.

*Author's collection*

**Chorlton-cum-Hardy, March 3rd 1958:** Many ex-GCR (and MS&L) locos led very long lives. Class J10 0-6-0 No.65144 was no exception having been built in 1896 and enjoying a working life of over 60 years. The J10's inclusion here is a trifle disingenuous: at the time it was allocated to the joint MR/GCR shed at Heaton Mersey (Stockport) and its appearance at Chorlton would be on a local pick-up (or "Pilot") working along the former Midland line and back to its home shed. Allan Brown's picture is probably one of 65144's last appearances on film; the loco was condemned later that month.

*W.A.Brown*

**We arrive back at Chorlton Junction, starting point for the Fallowfield line, to have a last look at two workings coming off the line en route back to Manchester Central.**

**Two contrasting scenes at Chorlton Junction: (Top c.1927):** The junction Branch Home signal beckons, but the station Distant warns caution as C1 Atlantic No.3272, then a Neepsend engine and the second of the class to be delivered- Doncaster, 1904 – comes off the Fallowfield line with a special working numbered 41. Taken from the signalbox, the photographer was the late G.H.Platt whose extensive photographic career began here with a box camera at around this time. *G.H.Platt*

**(Below 1947):** B1 No.1161 joins CLC metals for the final 3½ miles or so into Manchester Central with a Down "Boat Express" from either Harwich or Hull. One of the eight celebrated Vulcan Foundry B1s that went new in 1947 to Gorton painted in LNER green; 1161 became the "property" of Arthur Orsler. Notice the Midland-style signalbox which controlled operations here around the clock, seven days a week (save for a brief shutdown during the 1926 General Strike) from August 12th 1889 until closure on August 1st 1971, *J.M.Lloyd/courtesy David Hadfield*

## OBSERVATIONS AT CHORLTON BY W.A.BROWN JULY 18TH – AUGUST 20TH 1942

Although railway photography was outlawed under wartime regulations, note-taking, too, could prove fraught. The late Raymond Keeley recalled being apprehended by Military Police for recording details of one his train journeys, despite wearing RAF uniform! A section of Allan Brown's wartime observations at Chorlton–cum-Hardy are given here. They provide a valuable insight into the pattern of traffic, much of it Woodhead-bound.

**18/7/42**

Q6 2269 on freight
K3 134 on passenger
J11 5255 on freight
Q4 6054 "
O4 6524 "

**25/7/42**

O4 6276 on freight
O4 6234 "
K3 2490 "
K3 1325 "
O4 6592 "
B17 2846 on passenger
J39 1290 on freight
K3 1387 on passenger
B9 6107 on freight
K3 208 "
O4 6215 light engine (LE)
B17 2847 on passenger
B17 2852"
K3 116 on freight

**27/7/42**

B5 5186 on freight
O4 6298 "
O4 6254 "
K3 2767 LE
J11 5291 on freight
J6 3571 on freight
(load 31 + brake van)
B7 5031 on freight

**28/7/42**

O4 6349 on freight
C13 5020 on express
Q4 6134 on freight
K3s 118&153 coupled LE
O4 6264 on freight
J39 3082 LE
K3 1158 LE
O4 6325 on freight
D11 5502 on Hull-L'pool

**29/7/42**

J39 LE
K3 4003 LE
F2 5777 LE
C4 5264 Hull-L'pool
O4 6236 on freight
O4 6203 "
Q4 5136 "

**30/7/42**

O4 6298 on freight
(load 46 + brake van)
B17 2869 on express
B9 6113 on passenger
(tender-first!)
B9 6108
B17 2864 (LE - ex works)
J39 2784 on freight
B16 2366 "
(load 42 + brake van)
K3 116 on freight
(load 31 + brake van)
Q6 2251 on freight
(load 47 + brake van)
K2 4638 on Hull-L'pool
K3 4009 on freight
(load 48 + brake van)

**1/8/42**

O4 6235 on freight
O4 6255 "
K3 2443 on express
K3 2761 on freight
B7 5462 LE

**4/8/42**

Q7 628 on freight
K3 4008 on freight
C1 3287 on express
J39 1129 LE
J39 1295 on freight
J39 1275 "
Q7 904 "
(load 46 + brake van)
J39 3091 on freight
B16 934 on "

**5/8/42**

J39 1272 on freight
(load 51 + brake van)
B17 2853 on express
B7 5458 on freight
O4 6341 on freight
(load 46 + brake van)
Q7 628 on freight
(load 42 + brake van)
O4 6257 on freight
(load 43 + brake van)
Q4 5044 LE
B7 5481 on freight
B17 2834 on Hull-L'pool
J39 3094 on freight
O4 6529 "

K3 3822 on freight

**6/8/42**

B17 2866

**7/8/42**

J11 5997
O4 6331
C14 6120

**8/8/42**

B17 2852 (loco painted black)
N5 5909
O4 6276
B17 2847
O4 5389
O4 6353 (large boiler)
J39 2976

**10/8/42**

J10 5838
K3 4008
O4 6325
J10 5090 & 5798 as pilot
O4 5399
O4 6210
K3 2455
K3 3820 (ex-Works)
C13 5029
K3 1396
K3 17
C14 6131
B17 2864 (loco painted black)
O4 6299

**11/842**

Q4 6134

**12/8/42**

J11 5247
O4 6341
O4 6254
D9 6033
B7 5475

**13/8/42**

J39 3098
K3 2765
O4 6641
K2 4632
Q4 5959

C1 4421
J39 1898

**14/8/42**

B17 2869
O4 6625

**15/8/42**

O4 6325
J11 5991
B17 2864 (on freight!)
J10 5090
B4 6097

**16/8/42**

O4 6188

**17/8/42**

J39 2692
C1 4441
J11 6004
J39 1287
J39 1898

**18/8/42**

O4 6252
B7 5458
J39 1484
O4 6307
K3 140
K2 4637
Q4 5048
J39 1287
D11 5501
J39 2971

**19/8/42**

O4 6326
J39 1463
J39 1287
B9 6108
O4 6337
K3 1158
C1 4425
J39 1274
B15 815

**20/8/42**
O4 6302, Q4 6132, J6 3560,
J39 3095, K3 159, J39, 2785,
Q4 6132, B7 5031